CONTINENTAL MOTORING GUIDE

All you need to know
for safe and enjoyable motoring
on the continent

QUILLER PRESS

PORT OF DOVER

1991

This book is published by Dover Harbour Board in conjunction with Vauxhall Motors Limited.

Written and edited by Paul Youden,
Corporate Affairs Manager,
Dover Harbour Board.

Designed and typeset by
A & H Johnstone, Advertising & Design.

Illustrations by John Berry.

Printed by GP Printers Ltd, North Devon.

Our grateful thanks to the following who have contributed photographic material, maps, charts and other information.

The Royal Automobile Club

French Railways

Champagne Pannier

National Tourist Offices of:
Austria, France, Belgium, Czechoslovakia, Germany, Holland, Hungary, Italy, Luxembourg, Spain & Switzerland.

First published for the trade 1991
by Quiller Press Ltd.
46 Lillie Road,
London SW6 ITN
ISBN 1 870948 51 3

Contents

Foreword

The independence of a motoring holiday in Europe is something to be enjoyed by the whole family. The ability to go where you choose — and when — rather than to be stuck in a hotel room on a wet or simply non-beach day makes for a better all round holiday.

The construction of a whole series of fine motorways stretching from the Channel ports across Europe has mean't more time in the resort and less time driving.

Driving on the right hand side of the road has become a way of life for many people year after year. Businessmen and holidaymakers can enjoy the freedom of the open road unlike package tours by air as it costs the same for one in a car as four!

Taking that Continental holiday or short break with your car avoids fog-bound airports and frustrating delays caused by air traffic control problems.

Your motoring trip across Europe will allow you to find unspoilt beaches, quiet valleys, roam the vineyards of France and Germany or enjoy the magnificent views of the Alps. No need to queue for buses, wait for a taxi or rush for trains. No limit on baggage and when it comes to buying souvenirs, well just pop them in the car boot.

Mainland Europe is one large country. Borders have virtually disappeared and only a roadside sign indicates you have left one and entered another. There may well be differences in language but wherever you travel you will find those who speak and enjoy speaking English.

The book is published by Dover Harbour Board in conjunction with Vauxhall Motors who sincerely hope the advice contained in ***CONTINENTAL MOTORING GUIDE*** *will allow you to enjoy a carefree motoring trip to mainland Europe.*

We wish you a safe and enjoyable journey and please. . .
DRIVE CAREFULLY.

BON VOYAGE

The road to Dover

Located at the extreme south east corner of England, the Port of Dover is the nearest crossing point to mainland Europe. Driving to Dover is easily achieved on a motorway system which links in with most areas of Britain.

The opening of the M25 motorway around London coupled with the extension of other motorways to join in with this London orbital road means that from whichever starting point you commence your journey, your drive down to Europe's leading ferry port should be comparatively easy.

If you are driving down from the north and east you will probably want to cross the River Thames at the Dartford Tunnel which then leads on to the A2/M2 motorway. To reach Dover from the west and north-west you will probably choose the M25 anti-clockwise which then connects with the M20 via Maidstone, Ashford, Folkestone and

The White Cliffs of Dover

then on to Dover for the last eight miles on the A20 arriving at the western end of the port. An inner ring road of dual carriageway standard at the town will quickly take the motorist to the Eastern Docks ferry port which is the main terminal from where most ships depart.

The A2/M2 road from the Dartford tunnel comes to Dover via Canterbury and is dual carriageway until a few miles from the port. Even so, the road avoids the town and arrives directly at the Eastern Docks ferry terminal by way of an impressive viaduct from the top of the cliffs. On a fine day the traveller can see the coast of France (and even Calais itself on a really good day) before even leaving Dover! From whichever point you are commencing your journey in Britain, always leave enough time to reach Dover. Although final check-in time is only 30 minutes before the ships depart, most travellers prefer to leave between a half and a full hour to

General view of ferry berths at Dover's Eastern Docks Terminal

spare before their ferry departure time.

During the drive to Dover there can be unforeseen problems. A flat tyre, delays at roadworks or perhaps an accident has partially blocked the road causing traffic delays. It may even be that last minute shopping is required if "Mum" has forgotten to pack something. Or perhaps you forgot to turn off the central heating and you want to spend ten minutes ringing a neighbour or relative to pop around to the house.

Frustration caused by delays, frayed tempers, and not leaving yourself sufficient time to complete the drive to Dover in a relaxed manner can in itself lead to accidents. The last thing any family wants before setting off on that European motoring holiday is an accident so plan the journey carefully and if you are driving from the north of England or Scotland allow time for rest or petrol stops.

Computerised vehicle check-in at Dover's Eastern Docks. Each ferry operator accepts traffic at particular booths

THE VAUXHALL CAVALIER. BUILT IN BRITAIN AND CURRENTLY TRANSFORMING THE MARKET.

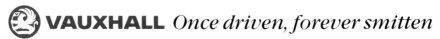

VAUXHALL *Once driven, forever smitten*

VAUXHALL IS BACKED BY THE WORLDWIDE RESOURCES OF GENERAL MOTORS. CAR SHOWN CAVALIER GSi 2000 16v.

As a guide allow one and a half hours to reach Dover once you join the A2/M2 south of the Dartford Tunnel or when you join the M20 at it's junction with the M25.

Dover is Europe's leading ferry port. In the main summer months from the end of May until early September there are as many as 90 ferry and hovercraft departures each day.

Of course, not all of these will be going to your port of destination because Dover serves four ports in Europe (Boulogne and Calais in France, Ostend and Zeebrugge in Belgium).

Most ferry services depart from the Eastern Docks. Ships for Boulogne, Calais, Ostend and Zeebrugge depart throughout the 24 hour period from here. Ticket check-in is simple and fast. If you have not got a ticket before arriving, computerised screens operated by friendly staff will show you at a glance the next departures to your chosen port and space availability. The chances are that even if you arrive without a ticket you could be on a ferry to France within an hour of arriving.

Within the Eastern Docks new road systems and large vehicle assembly parks have made life a lot easier for the traveller. Large signs marking routes "A", "B" or "C" lead the driver direct to his departure car lane. At the Ticket Check Point he will have been given a slip of paper indicating which route to follow.

With time to spare before departure — and shipping company staff indicate what time a ferry will be loading — the motorist and his family can take advantage of getting a warm (or cold) drink, a snack or browsing around the shops. Maps, tapes, batteries, car accessories, magazines, pre-packed sandwiches and gifts are all available in the complexes known as Welcome Break and Barnacles.

For those who prefer just to sit in the car, there is plenty of activity to watch before boarding your ship.

Ferries are arriving and departing all the time. The chances are you will have arrived before your ship (turn-round time for a ferry is only one hour) so you see the ship arrive at the ferry berth which is normally facing the vehicle assembly lanes where you are parked. From double deck, double width ramps, you will see cars, coaches, motor cycles and freight vehicles drive out of the ship. A full load can be discharged within 10/15 minutes. The crew on board are busily cleaning the ship and preparing it for the people about to drive on board. Loading is normally commenced about 20 minutes before the ship departs so if you have gone off for a drink or a browse around the shops, make sure you return to your vehicle before the appointed loading time.

During the second half of 1991 Hoverspeed will be operating a new service out of Dover. This will be the

EASTERN DOCK, DOVER...

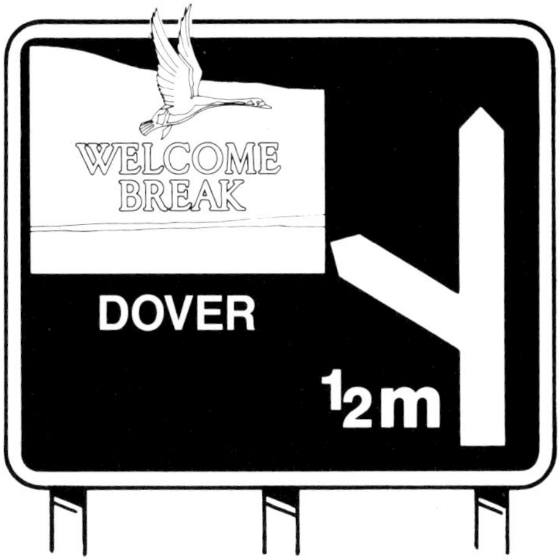

YOUR VERY LAST CHANCE OF A BRAND NEW WELCOME BREAK!

So don't miss out. Seize the opportunity to savour a relaxed interlude in genuinely pleasant surroundings. All the famous Welcome Break features are here for your enjoyment: a wide and appetising choice of food in our Granary Restaurant. Shopping for books, tapes or last minute necessities. A bar, a bureau de change and of course sparkling washrooms. In fact, you'll find that, like all Welcome Break service areas nationwide, we have what it takes to put you and your car in the best of shape, ready to take the continent by storm.

WELCOME BREAK

NOW OPEN

wave-piercing SeaCat with each craft capable of carrying 84 cars and nearly 400 people. As catamarans require traditional berths, the service will operate from the Eastern Docks and not the Hoverport. Full details can be obtained from Hoverspeed or from Dover Harbour Board.

Dover International Hoverport

If you have any questions or you require help while at the Eastern Docks, staff from either Dover Harbour Board, a shipping operator or the motoring organisations are always on hand.

Many people travel across the Channel by hovercraft and the terminal is located at the western end of the port. The hoverport is clearly signposted whether you arrive at Dover by way of the A2 or A20 roads. Departures are to Calais and Boulogne and there are as many as 29 daily during the main holiday months with the first flight leaving before 07.00 hours. The terminal is a "dedicated one" operated only by Hoverspeed and their staff will greet you, check-in the vehicle and then you usually have time to go into the terminal building for some light refreshments or visit the tax and duty-free shops. The building is modern and designed along an airport style principle and provides the traveller with telephones and a shop selling magazines, cassettes and gifts.

There is absolutely no reason why the disabled motorist cannot enjoy driving in mainland Europe in the same way as other motorists do. There are obviously a few differences and a few details to organise prior to the trip and this chapter is designed to assist the disabled motorist on his journey through the Port of Dover, his time on the ferry and, indeed, the facilities that exist generally throughout Europe.

THE PORT OF DOVER

On entering Dover Eastern Docks disabled drivers are well catered for. At the checkpoint there is a sign "Happy to Help" which is especially displayed for the disabled motorist. From this point you are issued with an orange sticker and informed which route you have to follow through the port down to the appropriate berth. There, Dover Harbour Board staff will direct you into your own lane to enable the shipping operator to direct you on to the ship to be parked as conveniently near the lift as possible. It is preferable that you give prior notice as this will enable staff to make the necessary arrangements without inconveniencing you in any way. There are ample disabled cloakroom facilities available throughout the port. Parking facilities have also been made available for you near the berths, free of charge, subject to availability, should you contemplate a day trip to the Continent.

Near the berths we have provided two self-service restaurants — Welcome Break and Barnacles — they are operated by Trust House Forte and, although they are self-service, THF staff are always happy to assist in any way possible. Welcome Break is built on one level and Barnacles has a ramp at one entrance to enable easy access to and egress from the restaurant. Again disabled toilet facilities are available.

Another plus for Dover Harbour Board is the installation of a "loop-system" at the port specifically to assist the hard of hearing.

New restaurant and shopping facilities at the Welcome Break, Dover Eastern Docks

P&O European Ferries endeavour to provide excellent facilities for passengers with mobility difficulties and to ensure that their crossing to the Continent is as smooth as possible.

They have many special facilities for the disabled, both on shore and

P & O European Ferries, Pride of Calais

in their ships — particularly their latest ships which have interconnecting lifts between lounges, bars, shops, bureau de change, restaurant, cafeterias, wheelchair accessible toilets and even cabins. Assistance for the disabled is available on all their routes, but some routes are certainly more convenient for disabled passengers than others. It is advisable to contact them when making your booking to be certain of getting the most out of their special facilities. They do request that you give at least 48 hours notice as this allows them sufficient time to make the necessary arrangements.

All Sealink ships operating out of Dover are equipped with lifts to assist the disabled motorist. Sealink require adequate notice of any disabled motorist travelling as their Movement Section ensure that all concerned, ships and shore, departure and arrival, outward and return are advised of the disabled passenger's crossing. Staff are always on hand to assist in any way possible. They make certain that the disabled passenger is put on an appropriate deck where he has access to the information office, cafeteria, bureau de change, bar, duty free shops, toilets and any other special facilities that may be needed.

Although their restaurants on board are all self-service, staff are always willing to help.

The Hovercraft service offers wheelchair facilities on site and disabled toilets are available. Passengers will also be assisted on to the hovercraft by Hoverspeed staff and no notice is required for this service.

MOTORING HOLIDAYS START ON BOARD WITH P&O EUROPEAN FERRIES

Motoring holidays start on board with P&O European Ferries which is sailing into the 1990s with a multi-million pound investment drive to turn your crossing into even more of a cruise.

The company's flagships, the luxurious superferries, Pride of Dover

and Pride of Calais, cross the Channel in just 75 minutes.

The ships, the largest and fastest on the Channel, can carry up to 2,300 passengers and 650 cars and operate from Dover to Calais.

Deluxe passenger accommodation includes a la carte and self-service

Shopping on board

restaurants, a shopping complex with high street department store-style shopping, a selection of bars and lounges as well as video facilities and children's playroom.

The cross-Channel leader also pioneered exclusive car ferry travel with the introduction of Club Class — on Dover based ships which travel to Calais, Boulogne and Zeebrugge.

For a small premium on standard single fare passengers can enjoy steward service, free coffee and tea and daily newspapers in luxurious lounges to get the holiday off to a good start.

The Duty Free shop sells not only wines, spirits and tobacco goods but perfumes, gifts and confectionery too.

The cruise-style Tax Free shops also sets new standards at sea. Lingerie, handbags, designer leisurewear — even ties and socks — are just some of the new lines of merchandise now available.

In addition, there is a greater selection of perfumes, watches, jewellery, photographic and audio equipment and travel goods — as well as P&O European Ferries own label — Blue Riband range of goods — on offer in the shop.

Playrooms for children featuring special 'soft' adventure play

Duty Free Shopping

equipment keep the youngsters amused during the crossing. Mother and baby facilities are available on all ships.

The cross-Channel leader also operates motoring holidays including ferry travel and accommodation to France, Belgium and Holland. Brochures are available at P&O European Ferries offices or ABTA travel agents.

Continental car insurance can be wrapped up in one easy transaction

Restaurant on board

with P&O European Ferries Green Card Plus which offers motorists unique benefits, including protection against loss of driver's UK no claims bonus and legal expenses cover.

Regular travellers can join the Motorpoints Club which offers gifts and travel discounts.

P&O European Ferries operate services from Dover to Calais, Boulogne, Ostend and Zeebrugge.

For bookings call Dover (0304) 203388 between 7.30 am and 19.30.

THE SEALINK STENA LINE EXPERIENCE

The year 1990 has seen tremendous changes for Sealink on the Dover to Calais route.

We believe that the two jumbo ships "Fantasia" and "Fiesta" introduced our passengers to a brand new era of luxury and comfort on the Channel.

A rich array of facilities are to be found on board these ships. There is an elegant and exclusive split level Motorist Lounge (see photo) with

General view of the motorist lounge on Fantasia

free of charge access to motorists; a popular discotheque under one of the most visually striking features of the ship, it's dome; an extensive range of catering facilities including a Pizza Counter and a spacious and well-stocked Duty-Tax Free shopping complex; a specially designed Children's Room, complete with a well appointed Mother and

Sealink Stena Line Flagship, Fantasia

Baby Unit and a vast sun deck for Summer trips which have all contributed to the outstanding popularity and tourist trade acclaim of the ships.

This leisure approach is a definite breakaway from days where only being transported across the Channel mattered.

The arrival of our Scandinavian owners, Stena Line, world famous for having pushed the full entertainment on board concept to a very high standard is adding to our firm determination to offer passengers the most pleasurable time on the English Channel.

This year one of the most spectacular results of the massive investment made by Sealink Stena Line to further the quality of service on it's Dover to Calais route, will be the introduction of a new £40 million purpose-built ship, the "Stena Invicta".

Together, Sealink Stena Line and their French partners, the SNCF, endeavour to give the best possible choice from Dover with up to 18 services a day at peak time, operated by four top class car ferries.

Whether it is for one of those very popular day trips to France, your main holiday, business or just a short break, Sealink Stena Line will offer, throughout the year, it's well known expertise, it's competitive rates and a whole range of special promotions.

You are very welcome to contact our Travel Centre at Dover Eastern Docks Booking Hall on (0304) 240280 for the latest travel information. Alternatively, your local Travel Agent will be pleased to acquaint you with our services.

Once on board, the Purser may be contacted should any special assistance or information be required.

Our Port staff, officers and crew look forward to welcoming you and we sincerely hope that you will enjoy the Sealink Stena experience.

HOVERSPEED — THE HIGH-SPEED CAR CARRIER

Hoverspeed, as the leading high speed car carrier, operates the largest commercial hovercraft fleet in the world.

The fleet comprises two SRN 4MK III craft, Princess Anne and Princess Margaret, each carrying 424 passengers and 55 cars. The three smaller SRN MK II craft, Prince of Wales, Sir Christopher and Swift carry 278 passengers and 35 cars.

Hoverspeed operates daily from Dover to Calais and Boulogne, up to 29 flights daily in the peak summer season and takes only 35 minutes to cross the Channel — twice as fast as the quickest ferry.

The company carries, on average 1.75 million passengers and 330,000 cars on over 9,500 short sea crossings from Dover to Calais and Boulogne.

Hoverspeed offers a variety of inclusive holidays and short breaks. Travel by any Hoverspeed route.

MOTORING HOLIDAYS — 7 and 14 night holidays with accommodation featuring villas, apartments, hotels and holiday villages to Go-As-You-Please touring holidays for the more adventurous. There are over 50 destinations throughout Europe.

The forest, the ruined castle on the hill, picturesque village and above all — good food and accommodation to be found in Germany

LE WEEKEND — Flexible Continental motoring breaks in France, Belgium, Holland and

Germany with a free audio cassette guide or travel pack to help you make the most of your time. Short breaks for 1 or more nights with accommodation ranging from comfortable 2 star hotels to 5 star chateaux.

SKI DRIVE — Skiing holidays with your car featuring hotels, studios and apartments in France, Switzerland and Austria. Taking your car means you can go where you like, when you like, take as much luggage and ski equipment as you like — and you can enjoy the scenery along the way.

CITY SPRINT — The fastest scheduled daily coach service from the centre of London to the centres of Paris, Amsterdam, Brussels and 12 other European destinations.

CITY LINK — A civilised and simple way to travel from the heart of London to the heart of Paris and the fastest surface journey between the capitals. From London Victoria to Paris Gare du Nord in around $5^1/_2$ hours.

For 25 years the UK and France have been linked by hovercraft services, operated first by Hoverlloyd and Seaspeed and, following the merger of those companies in 1981, by Hoverspeed. In 1986 Hoverspeed became part of the Sea Containers Group and is now spearheading that company's fast ferries activity. At the start of a new decade Hoverspeed is pioneering a new era of fast cross channel transportation by introducing the SeaCat wave piercing catamaran technology.

The SeaCats are the first craft of it's type to carry cars and Hoverspeed plan to begin introducing the craft on to the Dover routes in 1991, ultimately replacing existing hovercraft.

Hoverspeed Seacat

"Our aim is to offer customers the best aspects of airline service and conventional ferry facilities in addition to faster crossing times. We believe that the travelling public will find it an irresistible product", says Hoverspeed's Managing Director, Robin Wilkins.

SeaCat offers spacious individual seating with service of drinks, duty frees and light meals, plus a separate lounge bar and observation deck.

SeaCats will now form the basis of a rapid expansion of Hoverspeed's high speed ferry activity and maintain the company's reputation as a cross Channel innovator.

Preparing for your journey

Preparing for your European motoring holiday means you must follow some simple, but nevertheless important rules beforehand. Failure to do so could lead to frustration — or at worst — a ruined holiday.

Whatever type and age of car you have, inform your local garage that you intend taking it abroad. If it is due for a service, then make sure this is done well in advance of the departure date. Often a service can bring to light problems that appeared not to exist before. Sometimes problems can arise a few days after a service.

Repairs and spare parts can cost more abroad than back home. In addition to a "spares pack" available from firms like SELECTACAR take out a European motoring cover from one of the main motoring organisations or from EUROPE ASSISTANCE.

It is also a good idea to take with you a list of garages that can deal with any problems that might arise with your car in the country or countries you will be visiting.

Advice on insurance is to be found elsewhere in this book, but you must inform your insurance company that you intend to take the car out of the country. They will send you a Green Card which is proof that your vehicle insurance has been extended to fully comprehensive for European driving.

You must display a GB car sticker on your car — stocks available free from the Port of Dover

Mapping your route is also mentioned elsewhere in the book, but try and sort out beforehand who will navigate and get fixed at the back of your mind some main route numbers you will be following.

Advanced preparation can be enjoyable, bring excitement to the household and bring that magical holiday date nearer. But don't try and cut corners and don't leave things to the last minute. Start assembling all that you will need well in advance.

CHECKLIST

Have a checklist so that items collected can be ticked off as you go.

Passport(s)
Tickets
Insurance Green Card
Vehicle Registration Papers
E111 Health Certificate
Money
Eurocheque card and cheques
Spare Parts Kit
First Aid Kit
Red Triangle
Maps
Phrase Books

You will need to display a GB sticker of regulation size on the rear of your car. Dover Harbour Board can supply you with one free of charge and, as a helpful hint, don't fix it to the paintwork. The corner of the rear window is much better as it will not spoil the paintwork.

You must carry a valid driving licence with you and a copy of your vehicle registration document. Sometimes at border crossings, and especially between France and Belgium, the police seem to delight in singling out British cars and asking drivers for this document!

Ideally each member of the family should have a passport. Passports can take quite a few weeks to obtain so if you don't have one — or the existing one is due to expire — make sure this is taken care of in plenty of time.

When packing your passport(s), pack it with the tickets and maps in the front glove compartment of the car, not in a suitcase at the bottom of the car boot as has been seen on more than one occasion. There is nothing more embarrassing than having to unpack the car to get the passport out — with a line of cars behind you at Dover's outward passport control!

You do not require visas for visiting western European countries. This includes Hungary and Czechoslovakia.

ROOF RACKS

Many families find that the modern car boot just does not hold enough. So they equip the car with a roof rack. If a roof rack is not loaded correctly, or indeed too much weight is placed there, it can affect the stability of the car. As a general rule, put the heaviest things in the boot and the lightest things on the roof rack. Ensure they are properly secured and cover them with a good quality waterproof cover.

When making stops for petrol, coffee or whatever, periodically check the roof rack is still secure.

HEADLAMPS

It is an offence to travel abroad without converting the direction of the headlight. Remember you will be driving ON THE RIGHT so the beam must be directed to the opposite side. You can purchase a masking kit. Alternatively, you can do it yourself with black (or blue) insulation tape. IT IS NOT NECESSARY TO PAINT THE GLASS YELLOW. Only in France do cars have yellow headlights and this regulation only applies to French people! Painting the glass yellow cuts down on the effectiveness of the headlights. It also means you have got to clean it off with spirits when you return from holiday!

You must carry a warning triangle and first aid kit in the car. That is the law throughout Europe and if you break down, the warning triangle must be placed at a reasonable distance behind the car to warn approaching drivers. Twenty yards is a sensible distance.

A set of bulbs is also a must in some countries so put it on your list. Another item worth considering is a small fire extinguisher. Electrical faults can happen to modern cars — it might be you come across someone else's problem and then you are ready with the extinguisher. It is better to be prepared.

THEFT

Never leave your car unattended with valuable items on the back seat. Even stopping overnight at an hotel or guest house with luggage in the car can spell disaster. And always carry passports, money, cheque cards and cheques with you. Never leave these items in the car. Consider an alarm system on your car or — better still and less expensive — is the KROOKLOCK "visible" deterrent which is available from leading garages and motoring shops.

ANIMALS

Finally to a very important point. Do not take pets on holiday abroad with you and certainly DO NOT BRING ANY BACK. It is illegal to bring animals into Britain without a licence. Penalties are severe. Fines of many hundreds of pounds are imposed and sometimes IMPRISONMENT. If you have pets, either have neighbours care for them or place them in kennels. Pets sometimes deserve a break, they certainly deserve to be well cared for at all times. PREPARE FOR YOUR HOLIDAY CAREFULLY, CHECK AND RE-CHECK TO ENSURE YOU HAVE NOT FORGOTTEN SOMETHING.

PASSPORTS

Each member of the family should ideally have his or her own passport. Under the age of 16 years a child can travel on a parent's passport, but before you arrange this consider whether the child is ever likely to travel with a school party, in which case he or she would be better off with an individual passport. While a parent can travel alone on a passport which includes a child, a child cannot use the parent's passport on his or her own. Similarly, a wife may also be included on her husband's passport, but she cannot use it on her own.

A full EC 'Common Format Passport' containing 30 pages costs £15, one of 94 pages costs £30, and both last 10 years. In addition to the appropriate form you will need two photographs, not more than 63mm x 50mm (2$\frac{1}{2}$"x 2"), one signed on the back by either a doctor, bank manager, MP or person of similar standing who has known you for not less than two years, who is also required to countersign the form. These are then sent together with the fee and required documents to: Passport Office, Clive House, 70 Petty France, London. At the present time you can obtain passport application forms from the Post Office.

Alternative documents are:

1. A British Visitor's passport, which is valid for Western Europe only and lasts for one year. It costs £7.50 and can be obtained at main Post Offices. Two passport-size photographs are required.

2. The British Excursion Document (also obtainable at main Post Offices) for visits to France of not more than 60 hours at any one time. It is valid for one month and requires one passport-size photograph, countersigned on the back for the full passport, and costs £2.

OVERSEAS ASSISTANCE

More than a third of the motorists who take their cars abroad on

RABIES

GOING ABROAD?

COMING IN?

Don't take pets out. Don't bring any animals in.

All animal imports must be licensed.

BRINGING IT IN IS MADNESS

MAFF

WHAT IS RABIES? Rabies is a terrible disease which can affect all mammals including humans. Once symptoms develop the disease is almost always fatal.

HOW IS IT CAUGHT? Humans usually catch rabies when they are bitten by a pet animal which has been infected by a stray or wild animal. Such animals are particularly dangerous for young children who may approach such 'friendly' but infected animals.

RABIES PREVENTION: It is illegal to import any mammals into the British Isles except under licence. EVEN THEN animals must be kept in quarantine for six months. It is hardly ever worth your while to take pets abroad with you on holiday or for short-term visits because of the expense and separation involved in the six-month quarantine on return.

THE SIX MONTHS QUARANTINE PERIOD APPLIES EQUALLY TO ANIMALS WHICH HAVE BEEN VACCINATED AGAINST RABIES.

As an island Britain has long been able to keep rabies out by strict controls on the entry of dogs, cats and most other mammals.

One isolated case would be bad enough but conditions would be much worse if the disease became established permanently in our wildlife. The slightest animal bite or scratch would be a cause for fear.

ILLEGAL ENTRY: Our quarantine regulations are designed to keep Rabies out of Britain but smuggling of animals seriously threatens the safeguards we operate.

ILLEGAL LANDINGS RESULT IN PROSECUTION with severe penalties. They include unlimited fines, up to a year's imprisonment and the possibility that the animals may be destroyed.

DON'T Take your pets abroad.

DON'T attempt to import animals illegally.

REPORT ANY SUSPICION OF ILLEGAL ENTRY TO HM CUSTOMS AND/OR THE POLICE.

holiday or business trips make the journey without any motoring assistance of any kind, according to the RAC.

And research shows they are twice as likely to call for assistance once abroad. RAC touring experts find this situation both 'staggering and incredible'.

Ken Glozier, head of the RAC's Eurocover Services, says: "It is hard to imagine why so many motorists taking their cars abroad should place themselves in such a vulnerable position and run the risk of a holiday being completely ruined."

"But what is more incredible, is they seem unaware of the risk of having to pay bills amounting to four figure sums, should they need rescuing after a breakdown or an accident".

And all these risks could be avoided — for the sake of a few pounds a day, the cost of having assistance readily available at the end of a telephone at the RAC's European Control Centre in Calais which this year handled over 4,000 calls for assistance.

The Centre is manned 24 hours a day by English speaking staff who are known as Incident Managers, and operate one of France's most up-to-date telephone systems.

Additional telephones take advantage of the French 'green' phone system — equivalent of our Freephone — and separate lines have been allocated for drivers phoning from outside France.

The phone system also enables RAC operators to conduct up to a four-way conversation which could involve a motorist, a garage, an hotel and a car hire firm.

This year computers were installed to speed up the handling of calls and dispatching assistance to stranded motorists.

Ken Glozier adds: "Our presence in Calais is now much more apparent and gives added assurance to motorists arriving in France that they can call on our Continental resources in the event of an emergency and for help and guidance".

There is a growing network of garages throughout Western Europe who are used by the RAC, and who display the RAC's European Service sign.

Driving on the right

For most British people heading for that first-time Continental motoring holiday, probably the biggest worry is overcoming the problem of driving on the wrong side of the road. Even seasoned travellers still have a twinge of apprehension when they drive out of the French or Belgian ferry terminal.

Everyone adapts very quickly and within a few miles, you begin to wonder what all the fuss was about.

Of course, no one is suggesting you are blasè or become complacent. One of the basic rules to remember is not to be too nervous, but once you have successfully negotiated a few road junctions, you will begin to have confidence in yourself.

At the present time whichever of the four Dover-linked ferry ports you use, there will be a few miles of driving on normal roads before the motorway network begins. It may be that you have chosen to avoid motorways in which case you will be prepared for all that goes with driving through towns and villages, single carriageway roads, bends and the like.

However, for the motorist who is going to use the motorway system to head south or east once you have successfully driven that first few miles then you can relax a little once on the motorway.

Generally speaking drivers in all European countries drive faster than we do in Britain. Their speed limits on motorways and through towns and villages are slightly higher than our own. If you are a driver who enjoys speed, then something in the order of 75/80 mph (120/130km) is usually within the law throughout Europe. In Germany where there is

Many continental towns, especially in France, do not necessarily display a speed restriction at the start of a built up area. This is signified by the place name

no fixed upper speed limit, but a "recommended speed of 130km (80 mph)", you will find Mercedes, Porsche, Audi and Opel cars often zooming past at about 100 mph. If you dawdle in the inside lane, you will find lorries passing at between 65/70 mph.

At the end of a village or small town the speed limit no longer applies when the place name has a red diagonal line drawn through it

Although our European neighbours drive fast, they are usually more decisive and have been used to enjoying better roads for much longer than ourselves. They certainly do not take kindly to the indecisive driver in a town who sits at a road junction, or worse still, in the middle of a junction, wondering which way they should turn! It might sound daft, but I have seen British drivers do exactly that and then wonder why there is lots of "tooting", wailing and gnashing of teeth from local motorists.

Most British drivers do adapt very quickly to local conditions, and if you are in a town and not too sure where to go, then stop in a safe place without causing traffic chaos and ask

for directions.

As motorists we all have something to learn all the time, and after a motoring holiday in Europe, you will certainly return a better and wiser driver. For the business motorist who is likely to spend a great deal more time driving in the city or town, then being armed with local town maps if you are unsure of where you are going on that first journey, is a sensible idea.

The Route Nationale 5 at the French town of Melun

PRIORITIES

Without good roads, communications break down very quickly. Our European neighbours have known that for years, so wherever you drive you will enjoy a fine network of motorways or dual carriageway roads. Along these roads are frequent stopping places. Certainly a bit more than your usual lay-by. Large parking areas usually with toilet facilities are a good place to stretch the legs and let the children run around and let off a bit of steam. The Europeans believe in frequent rest stops — every three hours is recommended — but if you prefer to make use of the motorway service areas, then you are in for a delight. They are usually large and clean, some have restaurants as well as cafeterias. Most have a play area for children and the garage shop usually stocks a good selection of toys, souvenirs, cassettes, magazines and sweets.

A typical tree-lined road in France. Quiet and "off the beaten track"

Apart from excellent roads, what makes driving in Europe a pleasure, is the reliability of the majority of other motorists. By the use of the rear and side view mirrors, they generally know what is happening around them, especially important before overtaking. If your car has wing mirrors, then certainly use them wherever you are driving. Also make use of the rear view mirror frequently to avoid the "blind spot" when overtaking.

Be prepared. A French Autoroute (A26 from Calais South) is indicated as being 500m distance

Historic towns and cities are usually indicated by the use of white lettering on a brown background, as in the case of Cassel which is off to the right from the Dunkirk/Lille motorway

INTERNATIONAL ROAD SIGNS

These signs are in general use in Europe but may not be familiar to British drivers.

Priority Road | End of priority | Intersection (priority rule applies) | Intersection with tramway | Approaches to level crossings | Use of audible warning devices prohibited

AUSTRIA

Diversion | Tram turns at yellow or red | Federal road with priority | Federal road without priority | No entry for lorries with trailers | Prohibited to vehicles carrying dangerous goods | Buses only

BELGIUM

BULGARIA

U-turn compulsory | Turn right or left | No parking from 1st to 15th of month | No parking from 16th to end of month | U-turn allowed | Road for private cars | Lane prohibited to lorries

DENMARK

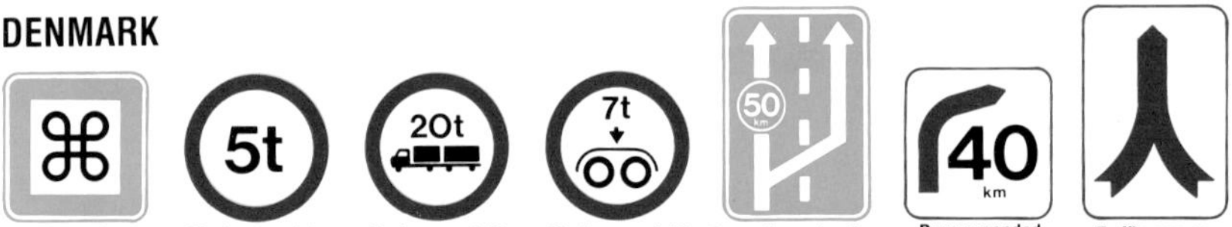

Sight-seeing | Maximum weight of vehicle or trailer | Maximum weight of vehicle and trailer | Maximum weight on double axle | Compulsory slow lane | Recommended speed in a bend | Traffic merges

FINLAND

FRANCE

Diversion due to road works | Prohibition applies between 0800 and 1800 hrs Mon-Sat | Prohibition applies between 0800 and 1400 hrs (Saturday) | Prohibition applies between 1000 and 1400 hrs Sunday | Keep well over to the right | Bus lane | Easily inflammable forest

EAST GERMANY

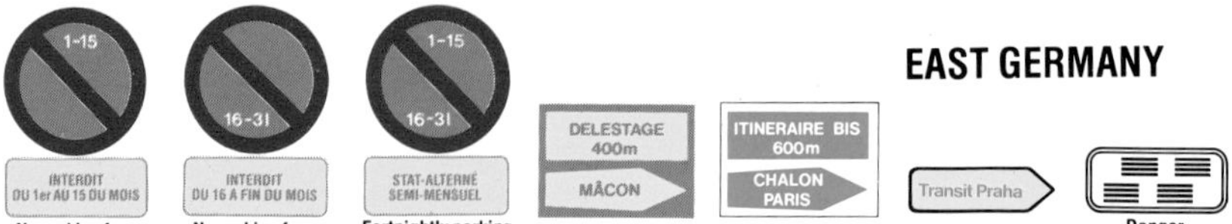

No parking from 1st to 15th of month | No parking from 16th to end of month | Fortnightly parking on alternate sides | Relief route | Holiday route | Transit route | Danger sudden fog patches

WEST GERMANY

Slow lane | Parking 2 hours (disc required) | Diversion | Street lights not on all night | Tram or bus stop | Emergency diversion for motorway traffic | Recommended speed range

Continued from inside front cover

HUNGARY

Diversion

Route for heavy vehicles

Lane reserved for buses from 0700 to 1900 hrs

Track for motorcycles

Road for motor vehicles

Restricted parking

Overtaking by vehicles with trailers prohibited

ITALY

Use chains or snow tyres from Km 174

Traffic in parallel lanes

Lane reserved for slow vehicles

No entry for pedestrians

Stop when meeting public transport bus on mountain road

Easily inflammable forest

NETHERLANDS

Cycle track (mopeds)

End of built-up area

End of B road

Crossing for cyclists and moped riders

Compulsory route for vehicles with dangerous goods

B road (width and axle weight limits)

No vehicle or combination over length shown

NORWAY

Tunnel

Parking 2 hrs from 0800-1700 hrs

Parking 2 hrs from 0800-1800 hrs (1600 hrs Sat.)

Parking prohibited (upper panel) Allowed (lower)

Sight-seeing

Road merges (black lane priority)

Passing place (on narrow roads)

PORTUGAL

End of parking prohibition

SPAIN

Recommended maximum speed

Take care (yellow or white triangle)

Turning permitted

Tourist office

Sight-seeing

No entry

Compulsory lane for motorcycles

Compulsory lane for lorries

Easily inflammable forest

SWEDEN

Maximum weight on double axle

Passing place (on narrow roads)

Tunnel

Slow lane

SWITZERLAND

Tunnel (lights compulsory)

Heavy coaches prohibited

Motorway

Semi-motorway

Flashing red light (level crossing)

Alternately flashing lights (level crossing)

Parking disc compulsory

Passing place for lorries

Slow lane

Trailers prohibited

Animals prohibited

Postal vehicles have priority

When approaching a frontier make sure you slow down in plenty of time. Maximum speed should not exceed 40km/h (25mph)

Road signs on German motorways are excellent, well spaced and give ample warning prior to an exit road

"AUSFAHRT" — means Exit on German motorways

The European driving test is stricter than our own, and in most countries involves a written examination in the classroom as well as the practical driving test. Also most countries do not allow a relative or friend to teach driving — you must attend a recognised driving school — so the end result is to turn out a better driver than we do in Britain.

When the first-time motorist thinking of that Continental motoring holiday asks the question "Isn't it difficult to drive on the right?", what is really at the back of his mind is: OVERTAKING, ROUNDABOUTS, GIVING WAY TO TRAFFIC FROM THE RIGHT, and THE RULES OF THE ROAD.

It is not necessary to loose sleep over any of these points, but each one is worth closer examination. Possibly with one exception, it is easier to drive on the right than on the left with a right-hand drive car which in several ways can give you an advantage over your European neighbour. You are able as a driver to judge distances between the car and the side of the road much better and tuck yourself nicely out of everyone's way while you enjoy the drive. On mountain roads, you haven't the width of the road to judge between you and the edge — a comforting thought!

OVERTAKING

The point about mirrors and the use of them has already been made. Before overtaking, make sure it is safe to do so and ensure you are not being overtaken yourself at the time you decide to pull out. Leave a sensible gap between yourself and the vehicle ahead. It is sometimes annoying to find another driver cuts in, maybe causing you to apply a little brake pressure, but sometimes he has only pulled over to let some fast idiot zoom by. If you are making use of roads other than motorways, then ensure you have a reliable person in the front passenger seat who can advise you on on-coming hazards, or alternatively, when it is safe to overtake. Such a person can be of considerable advantage, and once you have established that working relationship, make full use of it. Decisive words such as 'GO', or 'NOW' or 'WAIT' are important, not somebody who says, "I'm not sure, what do you think?" so you pull out and you find a 40-ton truck about to do a "paint job" on your front bonnet!

When driving on European motorways or dual carriageways, there are few problems, providing you make use of the mirrors and allow sufficient braking distance. Remember, at speed the car requires longer to stop. Accidents do happen on motorways, so please ensure you don't become part of a statistic.

On busy two-lane roads watch out for the international "No Overtaking" sign. Cars — one red and the other black alongside each other within a circle. Also overtaking when there is a continuous solid white line is forbidden. The line has been put there for a purpose so

A main road in France is indicated by a yellow diamond on a white background

observe it. It is an offence to cross and it is no use pleading British ignorance. European police impose on-the-spot fines. Many speak English and don't take kindly to someone trying to pull the wool over their eyes. For the sake of a few minutes, stay back until it is both safe and legal to overtake.

Remember also to let the driver behind know your intentions. Make full use of your traffic indicators. This applies to motorway as well as ordinary road driving. Apply the indictor in good time (having first ensured it is safe to pull out) and once you have overtaken use the right hand indicator to signal your intention of pulling back to the inside lane. Do not hog the outside lane. On three lane roads, you can legitimately make use of the centre lane PROVIDING the inside lane is being used by slow moving traffic such as lorries.

In most countries, traffic on a main road will have the right of way unless there is a sign to the contrary such as PRIORITE A DROITE. Normally, priority roads are marked periodically with the international priority sign of a red diamond. In France, they have a black on yellow diamond lozenge. In French towns they allow traffic from the right to have priority — a most unnerving experience for the British motorist — until you have got used to the idea.

Intersections require particular care and if you intend making a left-hand turn then don't forget to check the rear view mirror before turning. Also remember to finish up on the right side of the road — literally. Remember the rule abroad — DRIVE RIGHT — so if you make a left hand turn on a road junction you will want to finish up on the right hand side of the road.

At some busy junctions you will encounter traffic from the opposite direction wanting to turn right — across your path. As a general rule you must pass in front of other traffic turning. In Italy, Switzerland and Yugoslavia it is a rule to do just that. So it is the opposite of what you would expect back home. In Switzerland you can turn left in front of traffic islands in the middle of the road and in Austria, when turning left, you pass in front of the policeman directing traffic — unless, of course, he directs you otherwise.

ROUNDABOUTS

As in Britain, traffic already on a roundabout has the right of way in Germany and Yugoslavia, Greece, Hungary, Poland and Rumania. In ALL OTHER countries the reverse applies. Traffic entering a roundabout takes priority over traffic already circulating. Remember, you will be using a roundabout in an ANTI-CLOCKWISE direction which may seem strange the first time you do it, but just slip into the stream of normal traffic and it will become comparatively easy. As you approach the exit you want from the roundabout, keep as far as possible to the right to avoid being blocked by priority traffic entering.

DRIVE RIGHT

In some large cities in Germany, Switzerland, Belgium and Holland, trams are still in use. Trams have PRIORITY over other road users and the law must be obeyed. Trams usually operate down the centre of the road, although the bus stop is at the side of the road. When a tram stops, passengers have priority to cross the traffic lane to reach the tram. To block the passage of one of these "iron horses" could lead to an on-the-spot fine as well as encountering the fury of the tram driver. Also, remember that trams have to be overtaken on the "inside" or right.

PRIORITY VEHICLES

In addition to trams, other vehicles which have priority are emergency service vehicles such as fire engines, ambulances & police cars. In France, you must get out of the way of street cleaning vehicles and in Switzerland the POST BUS has priority on mountain roads. The drivers of these buses are experts and are used to mountain roads, however narrow. To warn other drivers of their impending approach, they

In Switzerland the Post Bus (PTT) has the right of way over all other traffic. This can be especially nerve-racking on narrow mountain roads

continually sound the horn. Perhaps a good piece of advice to heed is: ALWAYS GIVE WAY TO THOSE PEOPLE WHO LOOK AS IF THEY DON'T INTEND TO.

Details of motoring regulations applicable in each country, together with international road signs and in general, the law abroad are contained elsewhere in this book and should be studied carefully.

One final piece of advice to ensure you DRIVE RIGHT is do not cut the time for the journey home too fine. There are plenty of ferry and hovercraft services crossing the Channel and for the sake of a safe journey, it is better to miss your ship, even by five or ten minutes than taking a risk and find you are spending a few weeks longer on the Continent, probably in some hospital bed without too much of a view.

Mapping your route

It is reasonable to assume that most travellers going abroad for their holiday know their final destination. There are others — growing in number — who prefer to tour the highways and byways of Europe. For both, mapping out a sensible route is essential.

Although the European mainland is covered by an increasing number of good, fast and modern motorways, even these can be confusing where two or three motorways cross. By only sticking to motorways, the traveller can also miss a lot of splendid scenery, enchanting villages and the opportunity of stopping to savour a meal in a traditional village restaurant. Not every journey is without mishap and sometimes an enforced stop means leaving a main road system.

So the message is quite clear. Map out your route and above all, go equipped with the right maps.

Motorways in France and Italy, together with some of the Alpine

VIGNETTE!

roads and tunnels of Austria are toll roads. German, Belgian, Dutch and Swiss roads do not operate the toll system. Having said that, the Swiss make an "annual charge" for the privilege of using their motorways and you either pay on arrival at the frontier (30 SF) or obtain your vinette (windscreen tax disc) from the motoring organisations or Swiss National Tourist Office before leaving England. (see Countries of Europe A-Z).

City centres can be confusing places at the best of times but if you go equipped with a map or series of maps covering those large cities you are likely to visit they can be most useful. Not only in finding parking places, but one-way systems can have you going round in circles for hours unless you have a map which shows you how to get out!

REST PERIODS

Rest periods are essential for any journey, whether it be on motorways or side roads. The more people in the car for example, the more "penny-spending" stops you are likely to encounter. Driving on motorways enables the traveller to cover considerable distances quickly. For example, the French allow a speed of 130 kmh (80 mph), the Belgians 120 kmh (75 mph) and in Germany there is no fixed upper limit (except where specified) but a speed of between 130/150 kmh (80/90 mph) as a maximum is suggested.

Motorway service areas are plentiful throughout Europe, so plan to drive for about three hours and then have a rest for coffee, a fill-up with fuel and somewhere for the children to run around and let off steam. (see Taking the Children).

Stop and enjoy a picnic at one of the many motorway rest areas set aside throughout Europe. This one is in Luxembourg approaching the capital

If you are taking the highways and byways, then you are obviously not going to cover great distances each hour. Nevertheless, rest periods are equally important and no one should attempt to drive hour after hour. Your reflexes become less sharp the more tired the driver becomes and if the weather is hot, then tempers become frayed that much more quickly.

Sharing driving is another good idea, especially if you have confidence in the other persons' driving ability. It may be your wife, brother or a friend. Establish an understanding before setting out and change drivers every few hours.

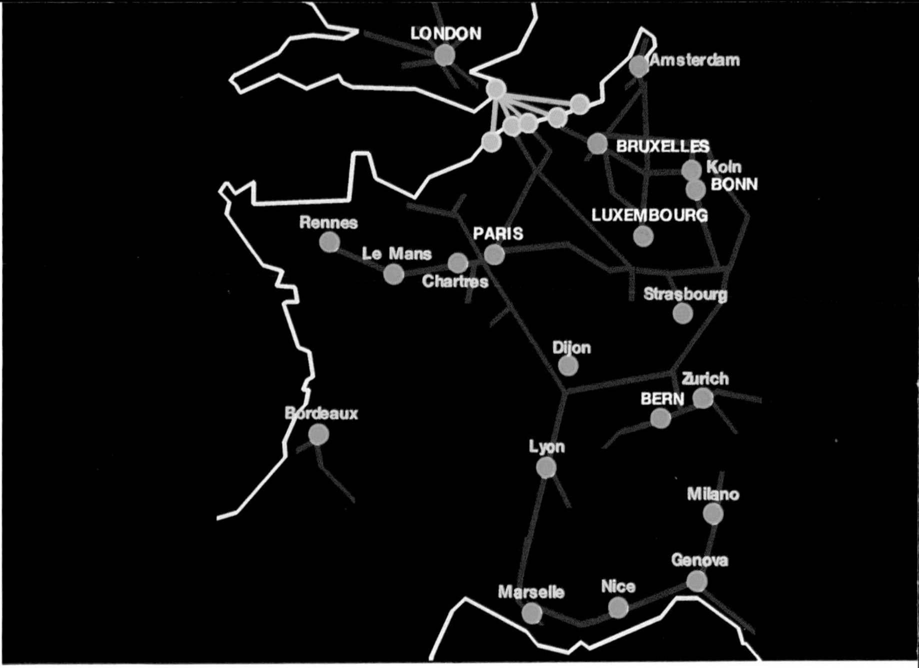

Map of main routes in France, Belgium and Luxembourg

The Black Forest region of Germany is delightful. Rivers, wooded slopes, picturesque villages and good food

If you are relying on another person in the car for map reading and have previously established that person knows how to read a map, then when they offer directions accept their advice. Do not have an argument as you drive along as this can easily lead to bad driving and perhaps even an accident if your attention is slightly distracted.

A Bavarian guest house extensively decorated on the outside with murals

Years of travelling throughout Europe and covering considerable distances each year, have convinced me more and more there is so much to see by taking a little time and trouble to stop and enjoy a view or an attractive village I had not previously known existed.

MAPS & GUIDES

Obtaining good maps and guides before you go on holiday, is important and it is advisable to have the most up-to-date available.

We recommend that these are purchased prior to departure, preferably when planning your holiday, thus giving you the opportunity of checking your proposed route and becoming familiar with the area in which you expect to stay. A route planning map is almost essential to get you to your destination, and, once there, detailed maps will help you find your way around the local highways and more importantly, the byways.

The excellent detailed Michelin maps suggest many local viewpoints along the way and what are considered to be scenic routes, as these maps are complementary to the well known green guides, the GB CAR CLUB have put together a series of 'Holiday Courier Kits' which include the Michelin Guide, in English, of course. Those for the French regions include the relevant route planning and detailed maps of the area. There are now two Normandy kits, Normandy West covers the Cherbourg peninsular and Mont St. Michel to Caen, whilst Normandy East covers Rouen and the Seine Valley, from Le Treport to Nogent-le-Rotrou. Every guide has a resume of the features in the area, with historical and architectural notes, crammed full of detailed information of the main and out-of-the-way places to visit and sights to see together with suggested itineries, both on foot and by car. Certainly a good motto is "Let your GB kit be your personal courier".

ITINERARIES!

One company who specialises in the supply of maps and guides with orders normally being dispatched within 48 hours, is The GB Car Club — see advertisement opposite.

CAMPING CARNET

No matter how you intend to travel, whether it is on foot or by train, cycle or car, if you are camping or taking your own caravan, you will probably find The GB Car Club's family Camping Carnet useful. This important document, is valid for up to 8 weeks without membership, provides personal identity and £500,000 public liability cover on authorised sites in Europe, and will normally be accepted at campsites in lieu of your passport. The holder must be over 18 years, some personal details with a passport size photograph will be required. See the GB CAR CLUB's advert opposite in this publication or contact the GB CAR CLUB at PO Box 11, Romsey, Hampshire, SO51 8XX. Tel: (0794) 515444.

A camp site in Northern France, near St Omer

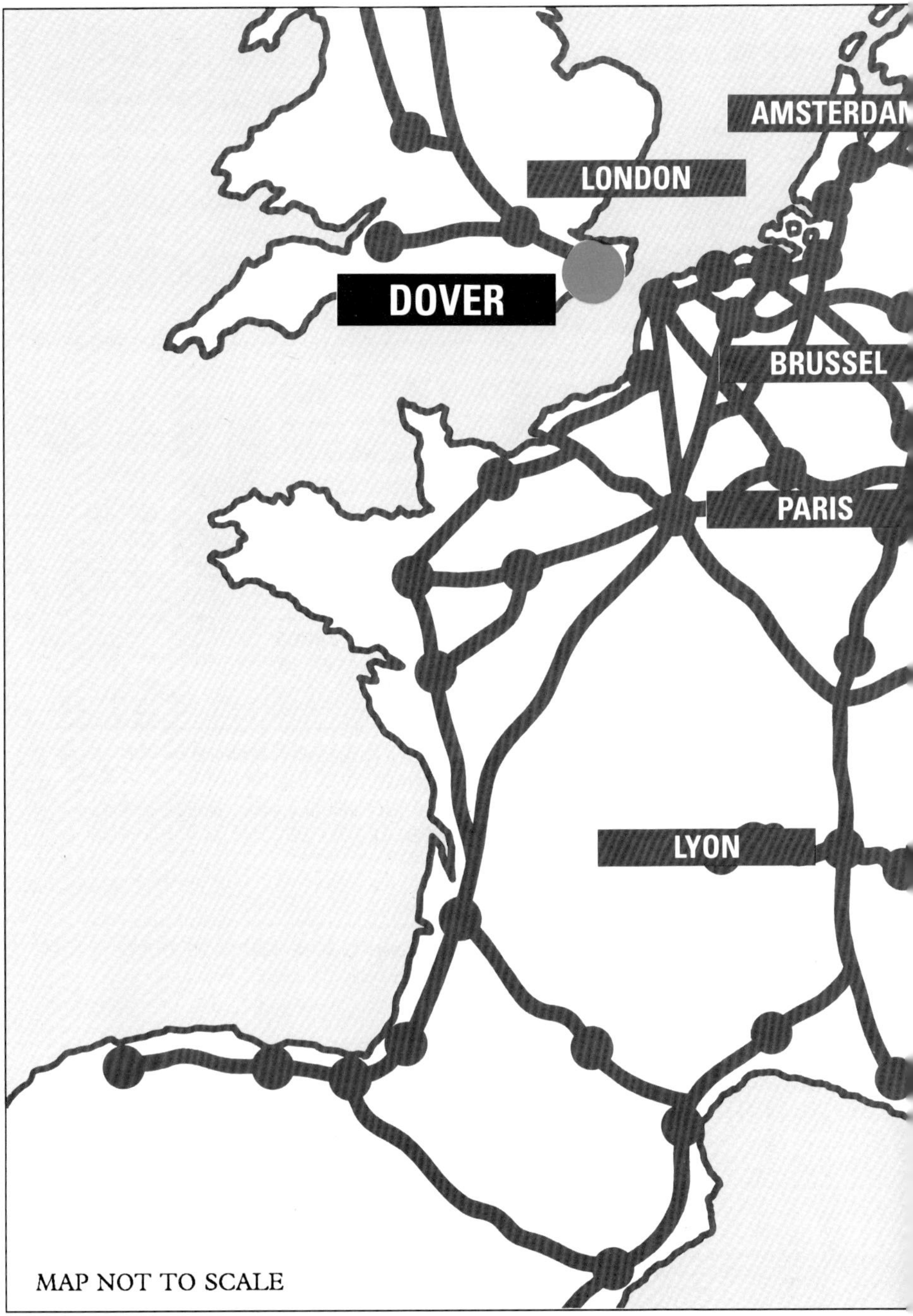
AMSTERDAM
LONDON
DOVER
BRUSSEL
PARIS
LYON
MAP NOT TO SCALE

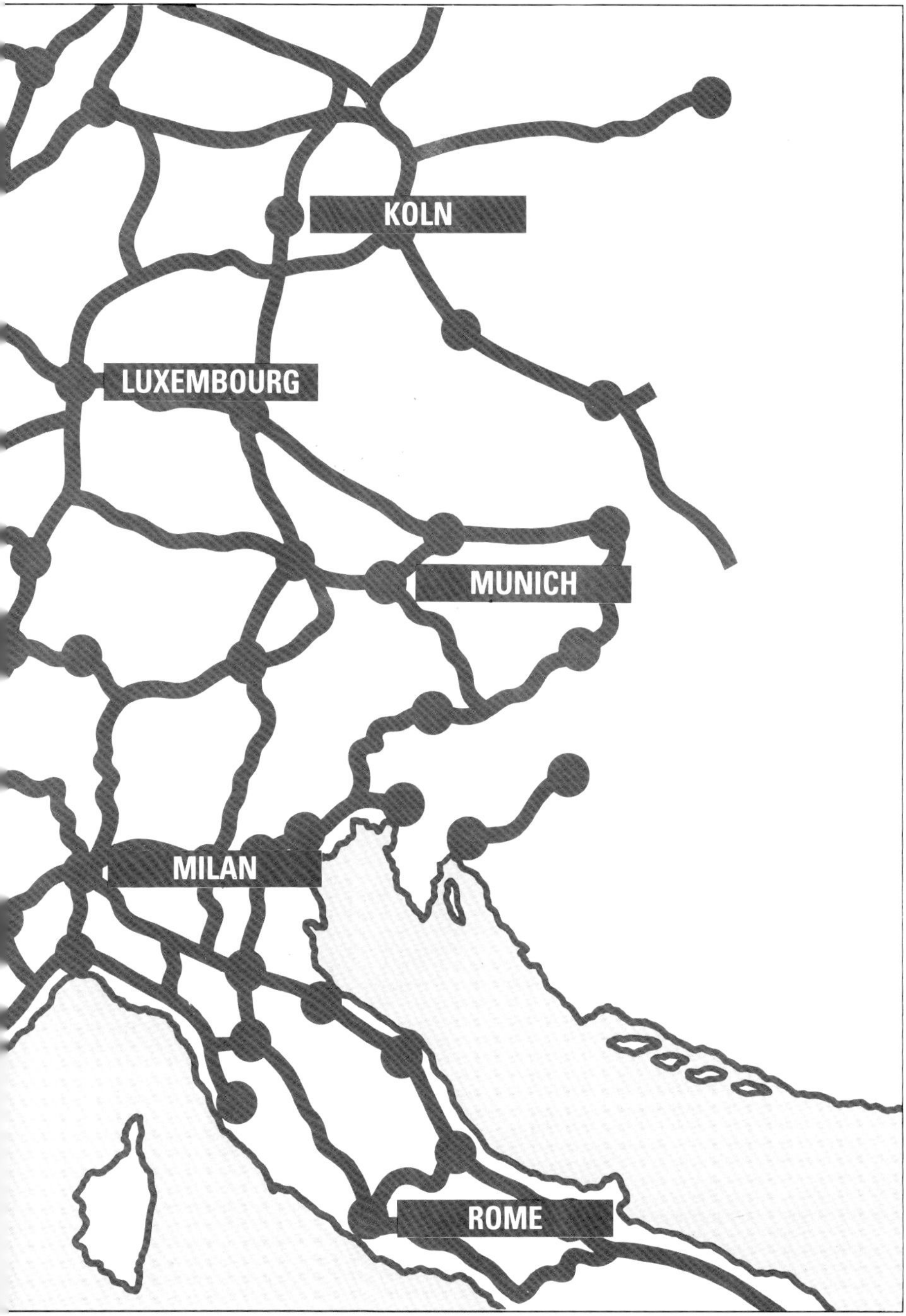
KOLN
LUXEMBOURG
MUNICH
MILAN
ROME

HOLIDAY TRAVEL INSURANCE

Wherever you go and however you travel, once the holiday decision has been taken, it is prudent to make sure that you have adequate Holiday Insurance. All too frequently, this is something that is left until the last minute or forgotten completely, with the 'It'll-never-happen-to-me' philosophy — unfortunately it may well happen to you.

If your holiday is one where cancellation fees may become payable, then it is essential that you have adequate personal insurance for all members of your party from the outset, certainly within 7 to 10 days of booking. Make sure that the policy you take out adequately covers these fees, and remember, most policies will exclude pre-existing conditions. Thus, if you leave it until later when you think you may have to cancel, it will then be too late to cover this event.

Although some people going abroad may be covered for medical matters by such schemes as BUPA and PPP, and American Express will replace their lost or stolen travellers cheques, it is still necessary to think of the other items that are not covered, such as personal accident benefits, loss of your luggage, handbags, wallets, cameras, jewellery, watches and actual money, or travel tickets, not to mention travel delay, (expensive items should have their own specific insurance cover), which, with difficulties to your vehicle are probably the major causes of holiday worries.

If you decide to holiday 'at home in the UK' this year, go Continental or trekking world-wide or even skiing, the GB CAR CLUB can provide inexpensive cover against

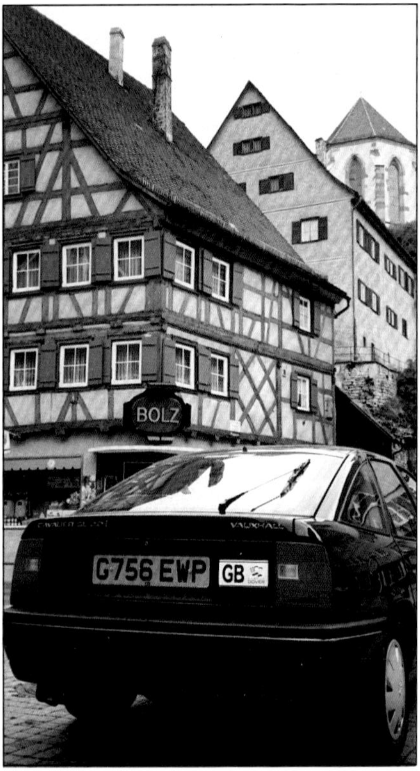

Attractively designed houses in a small town on the edge of the Black Forest

your holiday mishaps. Our skiing policy covers equipment and piste closure as well!

This is one reason why the GB CAR CLUB recommend their

Lloyds of London backed Travel Insurance or Motorsafe policies, another reason is that the insurance cover is very cost effective, with discounts for children and is probably the best in Europe.

To find out more, send a stamped addressed envelope to: The GB MOTOR CLUB, PO Box 11, Romsey, Hampshire, SO51 8XX for their 1991 brochure.

OVERNIGHTS

Long distances will probably require the traveller one or more overnight stops, especially, as an example, you are heading for the South of France, Spain, Southern Italy or Eastern Bavaria and Austria. Mapping your route will enable you to select a quiet village where you will find an inn or guest house not only offering good food and comfortable sleeping accommodation, but also a quiet location where you can really relax and recover from the previous day's driving.

Hospitality is normally good, friendly and value for money. Again, if you do not have personal knowledge or recommendations from friends, seek the help and advice of those in the "know". The national tourist offices can help and will send you brochures and even recommendations especially if you know in advance where you want to stop.

The Routier chain of family-run establishments has always been good value for money in France, and the Routier Guide is an excellent idea. It even covers Routier establishments located in countries other than France.

A typical Auberge in France. The Au Relais, which also offers accommodation is located on the N39 Hesdin to Montreuil road

Every country has it's family-owned guest house or restaurant. From Switzerland to Germany. From Austria to Holland you would have to be most unlucky not to strike it lucky. If you have friends or relatives who might be able to offer personal recommendations, then seriously consider taking their advice.

PLANNING

Having obtained the necessary maps and worked out the average mileage you will achieve having crossed the Channel from Dover prepare yourself an easy-to-follow list of route numbers and town/village names to look out for. This is also something to keep the children occupied with (see Taking the children).

MOTORWAYS FROM CALAIS TO THE SOUTH

MOTORWAYS FROM CALAIS TO GERMANY & CZECHOSLOVAKIA

1. CALAIS A26/E15
2. ARRAS A26/E17
3. ST QUENTIN A26/E17
4. REIMS A4/E17
5. METZ A4/E25
6. TO SAARBRUCKEN A32/E50
7. KAISERSLAUTERN A6/E50
8. HEILBRONN A6/E50
9. NURNBERG & AMBERG

MOTORWAYS FROM PARIS TO BRITTANY

1. PARIS A11/E50
2. CHARTRES A11/E50
3. LE MANS A81/E50
4. RENNES — BRITTANY AREA

MOTORWAYS FROM CALAIS TO NORTH, EAST OR SOUTH EUROPE

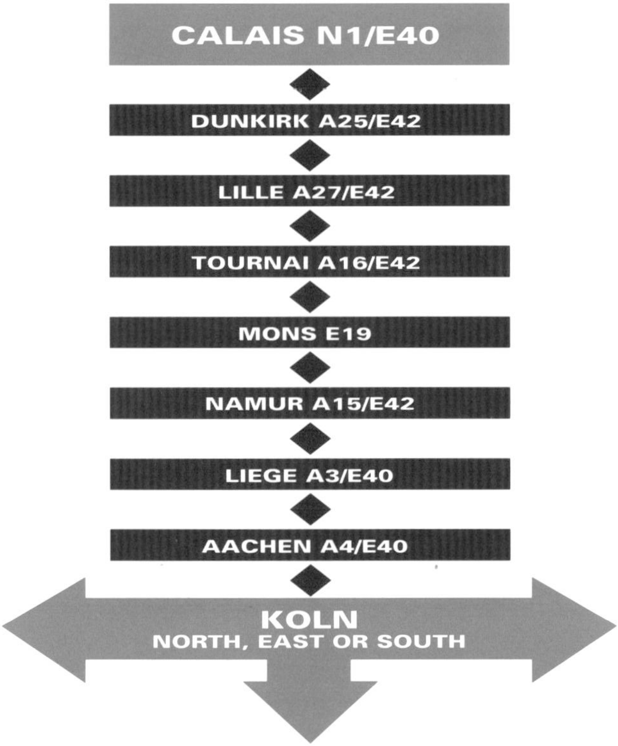

MOTORWAYS FROM NAMUR TO VOSGES

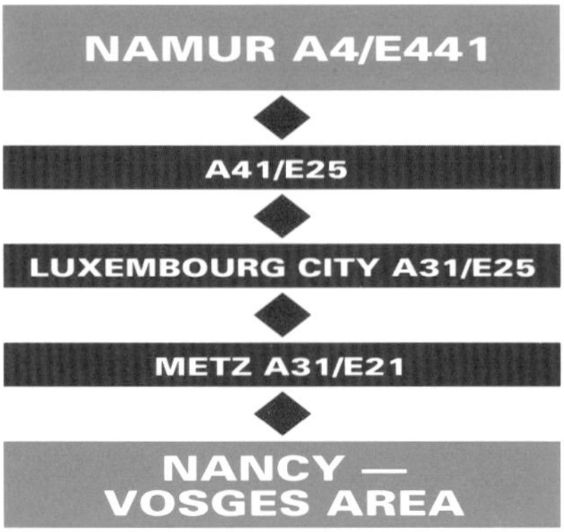

Driving abroad means DRIVING ON THE RIGHT. (TENEZ LA DROIT) in France or (RECHTS FAHREN) in German speaking countries. Whether you are a first time traveller to the Continent of Europe or a seasoned Continental driver, remembering to keep to the "wrong side" is naturally important. Advice for this can be found under the Driving on the right chapter, but it is worth reminding readers that the driver should never be distracted. Driving in towns, villages, coming out of car parks and even garages after a fill-up requires complete concentration. So establish some ground rules amongst those in the car, and let the driver get on with what is paramount to a successful holiday. A trouble-free and safe drive.

GET INSURED

When you are taking your car abroad it is always well worthwhile taking time to check your insurance arrangements. It may seem dull compared with the excitement of

The freedom of the open road does not always have to mean on motorways. Country roads can be quiet as well as straight and take the motorist through picturesque countryside

Tree-lined roads are a feature of France

planning your route, where to stay, etc., but your whole journey or holiday would be ruined if you became involved in an accident without adequate insurance cover.

Every motor policy in each of the EC member states automatically extends to give the minimum legal requirements of any other EC country. If you intend driving within mainland Europe, you should tell your insurance company, broker or agent two or three weeks beforehand and they will supply you with an International Motor Insurance Card (Green Card) which is evidence that you have complied with the minimum legal motor insurance requirements. Remember — the Green Card itself does not extend your insurance cover in any way, it merely gives proof that you have the minimum insurance required by law.

You will probably wish to extend the full level of your UK insurance cover to give you equivalent cover overseas. For example, if you have comprehensive cover, you will want this while you are abroad. If so, you may have to pay an additional premium.

If you do become involved in an accident while you are abroad you should report it immediately to the local Green Card Bureau, whose address will be on the Card. You should also report to your insurance company representative in the country concerned (your insurers can supply this when you extend your cover) and your own insurance company on return.

When your Green Card is delivered, you may also be issued with a form, a "European Accident Statement", which enables drivers to exchange facts quickly whilst events are still fresh in their minds without admitting liability. This document is widely used in Europe, and as an added help it is written in several languages to avoid communication problems if you and the other motorist don't speak the same language!

If you are travelling in Spain, the Spanish legal system requires the authorities to detain you and/or your car following an accident unless a deposit is made against the possibility of your being found responsible for the accident and fined. For a small additional cost, your insurers can supply a Bail Bond which acts as surety of these fines to supplement the minimum level of cover required by law. Ask for this when requesting an extension of cover and a Green Card.

It is a condition of all insurance policies that you take reasonable care of your property, so you must try to protect your car and it's contents against theft. It is as important as protecting your other possessions, particularly as it is your means of getting home. Don't forget to lock all doors, close windows and sun roof, lock your boot and do not leave valuables in your car. Remember, leaving a window or sun roof open because it is hot might make the car more comfortable, but could attract thieves.

Finally, do not forget to take out travel insurance to cover the other problems you might experience abroad, such as medical expenses for injuries or sickness, personal liability, travel delays, loss or damage to your baggage. Policies are available from travel agents, insurance brokers, intermediaries and direct from insurance companies. If a package travel policy does not seem suitable it may be possible to buy a selective cover for some risks only. Do remember to ask to see a specimen copy of the policy so that you are fully aware of the cover.

The Association of British Insurers offers a free leaflet "Holiday Insurance" which contains a section on motoring abroad.

Association of British Insurers,
Aldermary House, Queen Street,
London, EC4N 1TT.

N.B. Please mark your stamped, self-addressed envelope "Holiday Insurance".

BBC RADIO KEEPS YOU IN TOUCH

Most regions of this country now have their own BBC local Radio — and all give local traffic and travel news.

This service is especially important to motorists as they head towards Dover to ensure they are aware of any major problems, and listen out to information about delays and diversions ensuring they arrive at the ferry port for the ship with plenty of time to spare.

The following list is some of these BBC Radio Stations, and their frequencies which you can usefully tune into during your drive to Dover, listening to other programmes and music as well as motoring information:

BBC RADIO BEDFORDSHIRE
104.5; 95.5; 103.8FM: 630 & 1161 kHz AM

BBC RADIO BERKSHIRE
104.1FM; 94.6; 104.4 & 95.4 FM

BBC RADIO BRISTOL
95.5; 104.6; 94.9FM; 1548 kHz AM

BBC RADIO CAMBRIDGESHIRE
96FM; 1026 & ;1449 kHz AM

BBC CWR
(Coventry & Warwickshire)
94.8; 103.7 FM

BBC ESSEX
103.5; 95.3 FM; 765; 729 & 1530 kHz AM

BBC HEREFORD & WORCESTER
104; 94.7; 104.6 FM; 819 & 738 kHz AM

BBC RADIO LANCASHIRE
103.9; 104.5; 95.5 FM; 1557 & 855 kHz AM.

BBC RADIO LEICESTER
104.9 FM; 837 kHz AM

BBC RADIO LINCOLNSHIRE
94.9 FM; 1368 kHz AM

BBC RADIO OXFORD
95.2 FM; 1035 kHz AM

BBC RADIO SUFFOLK
103.9; 104.6 FM

BBC RADIO SUSSEX
104.5; 104; 95.3; 95.1 FM; 1161 & 1368 kHz AM

BBC RADIO WM
(West Midlands)
95.6 FM; 838 kHzAM

BBC RADIO KENT
104.2 & 96.7 FM; 774; 1035 & 1602kHz AM

Radio Kent is obviously very important during the last leg of your journey to Dover and provides travel at ten and twenty minute past each hour; twenty minutes and ten minutes to each hour.

Once across the Channel keeping in touch with events back home can be achieved by listening to BBC Radio World Service. Very few

EUROPEAN DISTANCE CHART

The chart here shows the distances between the European capitals in kilometres.

	AMSTERDAM	ATHENS	BARCELONA	BELGRADE	BERLIN	BONN	BRUSSELS	BUCHAREST	BUDAPEST	CALAIS	DUBLIN	FRANKFURT aM	GENEVA	HAMBURG	ISTANBUL	COPENHAGEN	LISBON	LONDON	LUXEMBOURG	MADRID	MARSEILLE	MILAN	MOSCOW	MUNICH	OSLO	PALERMO	PARIS	PRAGUE	ROME	STOCKHOLM	STRASBOURG	WARSAW	VIENNA	ZURICH
AMSTERDAM																																		
ATHENS	2940																																	
BARCELONA	1585	3400																																
BELGRADE	1785	1155	2075																															
BERLIN	690	2450	1885	1290																														
BONN	325	2715	1450	1495	600																													
BRUSSELS	200	2960	1385	1775	790	155																												
BUCHAREST	2385	1230	2635	605	1740	2090	2310																											
BUDAPEST	1440	1550	2000	395	900	1255	1175	835																										
CALAIS	355	3180	1385	1965	1000	370	215	2525	1690																									
DUBLIN	880	3895	2000	2665	1715	1085	930	3240	2405	715																								
FRANKFURT aM	455	2540	1315	1275	540	180	400	1930	985	615	1330																							
GENEVA	945	2600	735	1415	1115	720	815	2020	1280	805	1520	575																						
HAMBURG	440	2920	1710	1765	285	455	630	2045	1190	780	1495	495	1070																					
ISTANBUL	2750	1135	3090	955	2250	2440	2730	695	1350	2920	3620	2230	2370	2560																				
COPENHAGEN	800	2740	2020	1760	455	765	940	2190	1360	1090	1400	805	1380	310	2715																			
LISBON	2275	4510	1280	3415	2890	2730	2075	3915	3300	2075	2790	2350	2015	2705	4370	3015																		
LONDON	340	3350	1455	2125	1005	540	380	2655	1860	170	535	785	975	950	3080	1170	2245																	
LUXEMBOURG	385	2710	1270	1560	790	235	215	2100	1230	415	1130	290	600	635	2515	945	2155	585																
MADRID	1750	3860	630	2765	2515	2080	1550	3265	2630	1550	2265	1825	1365	2200	3720	2510	650	1720	1630															
MARSEILLE	1255	2730	500	1635	1540	1145	1065	2135	1500	1065	1780	1000	425	1495	2590	1805	1780	1235	920	1130														
MILAN	1180	2205	1025	1045	1160	980	915	1610	975	1130	1845	675	325	1170	2000	1480	2305	1300	700	1655	525													
MOSCOW	2520	3070	3575	2240	1835	2435	2630	1835	2065	2835	3550	2400	2825	2120	2525	2090	4855	3000	2620	4205	3340	2740												
MUNICH	855	2140	1330	985	585	560	780	1530	695	925	1640	400	585	780	1940	1090	2600	1100	570	1950	1020	575	2240											
OSLO	1400	3515	2525	2350	1060	1270	1445	2805	2040	1600	1440	1310	1885	860	3305	600	3520	1700	1545	3060	2355	2030	2075	1640										
PALERMO	2740	1570	2450	1500	2605	2460	2380	2135	1895	2670	3385	2220	1800	2700	2120	3010	3700	2840	2280	3020	1950	1530	4045	1880	3520									
PARIS	470	3055	1085	1805	1115	510	300	2375	1540	300	1015	575	505	930	2760	1240	1775	470	365	1250	765	830	2915	830	1790	2370								
PRAGUE	970	2120	1700	935	355	680	850	1380	570	1130	1845	515	950	640	1920	810	2815	1300	745	2315	1390	940	1875	365	1420	2245	1040							
ROME	1780	1410	1385	1295	1505	1500	1420	1670	1210	1710	2415	1260	910	1740	1985	2050	2660	1880	1270	2010	990	570	3085	920	2560	960	1410	1285						
STOCKHOLM	1425	3575	2620	2375	1100	1385	1580	2720	1500	1740	1870	1445	2020	950	3330	640	3655	1810	1635	3150	2445	2120	1535	1730	540	3650	1880	1455	2650					
STRASBOURG	670	2525	1125	1370	750	360	440	1890	1055	600	1315	220	390	715	2325	1025	2200	770	220	1755	815	490	2425	360	1530	2020	490	610	1060	1665				
WARSAW	1270	2260	2325	1105	585	1185	1375	1380	710	1585	2300	1140	1575	870	2020	840	3440	1755	1370	2940	2015	1490	1250	990	1480	2560	1665	625	1800	935	1235			
VIENNA	1190	1805	1770	650	650	1000	920	1090	255	1340	2055	730	1025	1110	1605	1105	3030	1510	1000	2390	1425	900	1920	440	1710	2090	1285	315	1130	1750	800	670		
ZURICH	875	2500	1020	1375	840	540	655	1850	1005	795	1510	415	275	920	2430	1230	2280	965	435	1640	700	290	2545	315	1780	1820	575	665	860	1870	230	1300	750	

people, however, know how to find their way to World Service and often spend two weeks of their holiday listening to foreign radio stations and reading out of date English newspapers.

Here are some helpful hints to BBC radio abroad.

BBC World Service is transmited around the clock and to receive it throughout Europe, your radio (car or personal set) should be equipped with SHORT WAVE (SW). A good SW set covering the broadcast bands between 5.8 and 18 MHz is almost essential. Long Wave (LW) coverage will give you Radio 4 in parts of Europe and Radio 4 LW channel is used daily by BBC World Service for a few hours early each morning. MEDIUM WAVE (MW or AM) coverage might enable you to receive Radios 1 and 2 in parts of western Europe. BBC World Service is also transmitted on MW band to some parts of Western Europe.

WORLD SERVICE
Frequency 648 kHz;
Wavelength 463 metres.

Reception of BBC Radio in Europe (World Service)

Austria SW
Belgium MW 648kHz SW
Denmark SW
France (central) SW
France (northern) MW 648kHz SW
Germany MW 648kHz SW
Holland MW 648kHz SW
Italy SW
Luxembourg MW 648kHz SW
Spain SW
Switzerland SW

BBC Radio 4 can also be found in the following countries:

Belgium LW 198kHz
France LW 198kHz
Holland LW 198kHz
Luxembourg LW 198kHz

BEFORE YOU DEPART

Plan your journey well.
Leave an itinerary with a relative or friend in case of emergency.
Cancel the newspapers and milk deliveries.
Get vehicle serviced.
Check passports are still valid until after you return home.
On receipt check details on tickets in case alterations have to be made.
Obtain Eurocheques and Eurocheque card from bank well in advance.
Obtain Travellers Cheques and currency from bank.
Obtain E111 for medical treatment abroad.
Organise house watch.
For winter holidays perhaps drain down the water system at home.
Turn off gas and electricity (? fridge).
Check tyre pressure and oil.
Check you have with you the telephone number where to report stolen or lost credit cards/cheque books.

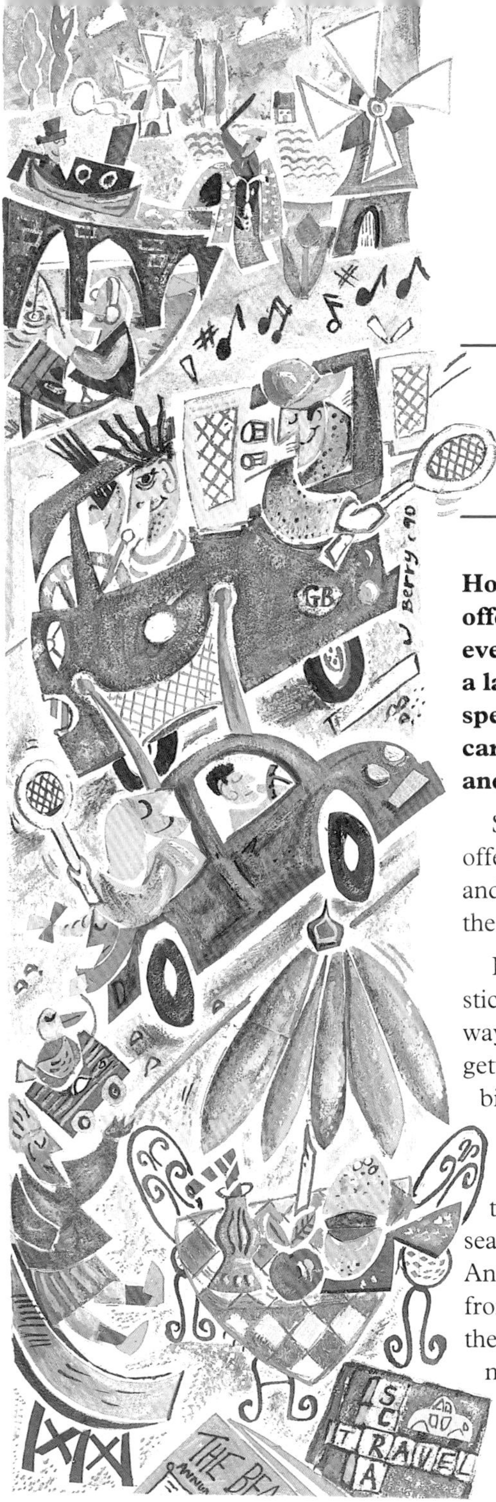

Taking the Children

Holidays abroad for children offer excitement, adventure and even the opportunity of practising a language. The prospect of spending considerable time in the car is daunting both for children and parents alike.

Some families go motorail which offers both the opportunity of a bed and the chance to walk up and down the train.

However, the majority of families stick to the car and many search for ways of keeping the children from getting too restless — or even bickering if there is more than one child in the back seat.

First-time travellers may wish to take heed of what some seasoned car travellers have found. And that is to take an evening ferry from Dover and then drive through the night. Children naturally sleep at night, they also usually sleep when it is dark. Add to this the fact that nights are less hot (even in summer) than the days and you have ingredients to allow you to cover quite a few hundred miles with quietness coming from the back seat!

Nobody is suggesting you can complete the entire journey to your destination in this way, and certainly it will be necessary to find children something to keep them occupied.

Driving through a French forest looking for a suitable picnic spot

Young children find it difficult to understand distances so the longer it is, the more easily bored they become. Older children can be kept occupied more easily by encouraging them to take an interest in what is going on. Allow them to map read, watch out for signs. Perhaps even write down the names of principal towns or landmarks and the distance covered between each. Another idea is to let them watch out for particular car numbers. Depending on which country you are in, there are systems of identifying where a car has come from. In France a number at the end of the number plate signifies which area the car comes from. "59" is the Nord Pas de Calais. Paris has the number "75 " and the Provence region "06 ". In Germany, it is the letters at the beginning of the number plate. "A" is Aachen. "B" Berlin, "M" Munich. Usually it is two letters so "SP" is Speyer. "KL" is Kaiserslautern, "HH" is Hamburg. And so on.

Perhaps you can offer a competition over say half an hour. Who can spot the most number of Vauxhall Opel cars?

In car entertainment for the younger child is something else to consider. Storyteller cassettes are good and can last up to an hour. Most cars have radio cassettes these days, but if not, carry a small personal cassette player and a teenager can find hours of enjoyment from cassettes. Mum and Dad may have different tastes in music so a personal cassette player enables the teenager to enjoy the latest "blasts" of pop without annoying Dad.

A firm specialising in a range of games for the traveller is supplied by Hasbro Bradley UK, and is marketed under the MB brand name. The MB range of travel games comprises 7 different games which can be played literally anywhere. Each game is compact and portable, featuring magnetic playing pieces and/or contained dice.

At the hotel, Mum and Dad will probably enjoy playing as well, but for the children travelling, the range includes GUESS WHO? BATTLESHIP, FRUSTRATION and CONNECT 4. Prices range from £3 to £5 and are an excellent investment.

Travel Frustration from MB Games

When travelling with children, frequent car stops are important. The further south you go, the hotter the weather usually becomes. Children need to stretch their legs more often than adults, probably toilet stops are more frequent. They also like to nibble. Dentists will tell you too many sweets are not a good idea, so how about a variety such as crisps, apples or other fruit, nuts and certainly plenty of drinks. There are a variety of fruit juices now available in small plastic containers complete with straw. Why not invest in a number of "six" packs for the journey.

As mentioned elsewhere in the book, Continental lay-bys are usually superior areas to those we recognise in England. They have large grassed areas, usually with some trees and toilets. Children's play areas are provided at most motorway restaurant stops so let the children enjoy half an hour of letting off steam.

Alternatively, as you head south, turn off the main road into a small village, particularly if it is in a valley and has a stream. A few minutes of paddling can be quite refreshing on a hot day.

For the very young children a pillow and blanket and their favourite cuddly toy is a must for the back seat. Don't leave behind their favourite "sucking cloth" as it will cause all sorts of emotional problems.

By law back seat travellers must wear seat belts in Europe (if fitted), and this applies equally to children. Safety is paramount on a motoring holiday and whatever objections children might first put up, it is essential the law is obeyed. A child safety seat not only offers protection, it also raises them up sufficiently high enough to see out of the window and what is going on.

CHILD HEALTH

If you have never taken your child abroad before and you know you are going somewhere hot, consult your doctor or chemist before you go. Even adults can suffer from upset tummies. A change of climate, food or drink can bring on mild problems. Talks of the "illness risk" are grossly exaggerated but a few simple precautions will save hours of anguish.

Throughout the Continent there is a more mature outlook on the involvement of children on holiday than we have in England. Children are encouraged to accompany parents to restaurants, even for Sunday lunch. Hotels and guest houses have "family rooms" and you pay for the room, not for each individual.

Unlike Britain, you can take children into establishments which serve alcohol and providing you don't buy your ten-year-old a gin and tonic or a malt whisky, nobody will think twice about the youngster.

Children like mixing and can make friends easily. Language barriers are quickly broken with a few signs, a smile and a simple understanding. However, do encourage children to try to learn a little of the language. Now that children from the age of 11 will be learning French, German and Spanish in school, it will help their education by taking them abroad. Equip them with a dictionary and a simple phrase book. Perhaps even a competition involving Mum and Dad to see who has learned the most new words or phrases each day.

Finally, if you are heading for a sunshine holiday to the south of France or Spain, Even perhaps Bavaria or Switzerland where summers can be equally hot, do remember that exposure to too much sun is bad for adults and children alike. Avoid the direct sun between 12 noon and 14.00 hours. Make sure children are wearing a tee-shirt and even a hat. Sunstroke is bad and can spoil a holiday. The long term effects of too much sun on the skin are now a well established fact.

Happy families on the beach

If the children enjoy swimming, whether it be in an outdoor pool or in the sea, apply a good cream. Anything from factor number 7 to 12 is a good idea. And if you are inland and the children are making use of a pool, apply liberal amounts of Autan cream or spray to prevent insect bites and stings.

Be Prepared!

The major worry for those planning a caravan holiday abroad is driving on the other side of the road, although this usually proves no problem after the first hour or so. The next concern is the standard of roads and gradients especially in the more mountainous regions of Europe. Take heart, as Britain has not only worse gradients on it's main roads than almost any other European country, but also a high density of traffic.

Plan your journey in advance and study maps and mileage charts before you cross the Channel, and if you are travelling in the height of the summer, it is wise to stop every couple of hours to stretch your legs, have a drink and generally escape from the heat of the car. This is especially important with young children in the family and is very easy on the motorways where stopping places are well signposted in advance.

CARAVANNING

Do be sure to have your car and caravan fully serviced before your holiday and take a well equipped spares kit with you (these can be hired either from your main car dealer or through your travel service). Also have a spare wheel and tyre for your caravan as the lack of one is probably the main single cause of a spoiled holiday. Cross ply tyres are not available on the Continent

Caravanning in Southern Germany can take full advantage of the excellent scenery and camp sites

and it is not permissible to mix crossply and radial tyres, so if you have a problem not only will you suffer delays, but also need to purchase two new tyres at once. You must fit a towing mirror on the nearside of the car and adjust the headlights to deflect to the right instead of the left using headlamp converters or beam deflectors (the latter are not suitable for use on quartz halogen lamps).

Once you are driving always look to the left and not to the right at a T-junction or crossroads or before entering a roundabout. Some people find it useful to stick a small note on the dashboard just to remind them that it is DRIVE RIGHT and LOOK LEFT. This is very useful when you have stopped for a rest as it is easy to forget that you are not still in the UK when first starting your holiday drive. Be careful when overtaking and ensure that the road ahead is clear by staying well behind the vehicle in front. It does help if your front seat passenger has good enough judgment to give the 'all clear'.

When you are used to driving in British weather conditions, it is easy to forget the possibility of overheating so be vigilant on long hill climbs and do not switch off the engine in queues when it is hot, but keep the fan running. Another point is that an engine can lose power at altitude which makes it labour on gradients, so try to take high passes in the cool of the morning.

For the caravan take a set of spare road light bulbs; this is a legal requirement in several countries as is a first aid kit (always advisable even when not mandatory). Most people go abroad to take advantage of the climate so an awning plus a folding table and chairs is a must for enjoying those alfresco meals without getting too sunburnt. Mosquitoes and flies can be a nuisance, so apart from some effective repellent

Camp sites can often be found in idyllic settings such as this one at St Martin, off the D225 south west of St Omer

MOTORAIL for MOTORISTS

The Expressway into Europe

New for 1991

- ✲ *MORE MID-WEEK DISCOUNTS*
- ✲ *NEW BOULOGNE-ROME SERVICE*
- ✲ *REDUCED FARES ON HOVERSPEED*
- ✲ *SPECIAL TRAVEL INSURANCE OFFER*

Why Travel Motorail?

If you have never travelled Motorail you may wonder why so many people, over a million in fact, opt for an overnight rail journey through France with their car (or motorbike) carried on the train, rather than driving all the way. Here are a few of the reasons:

You save 2 days' holiday:

Do you really want to spend 4 days out of 14 driving there and back? By sleeping while you travel, you save a whole day in each direction.

You cut out the long, tiring drive:

Give your nerves a rest. With Motorail you avoid the rigours of the motorway and you arrive relaxed. It's a lot safer, too!

You can even save money:

Just compare the cost of Motorail with driving, taking into account the price of petrol, motorway tolls, hotels, restaurants and wear and tear on the car. Moreover, when you book Motorail, you get special reduced cross-Channel fares on Sealink, P&O and Hoverspeed. The chances are that Motorail is the cheaper alternative – ask your motoring organisation if you don't believe it.

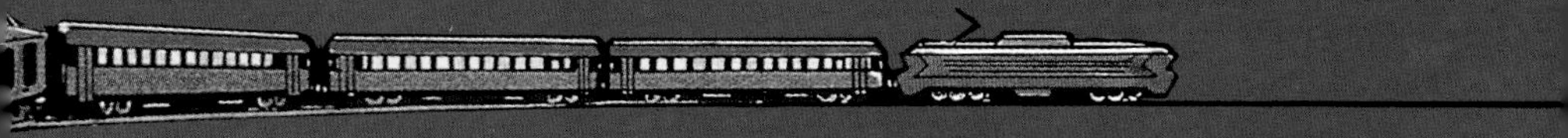

For further information and bookings contact
French Railways Ltd, 179 Piccadilly, London W1V 0BA.
Tel. 071-409 3518. 24 hour Brochure Hotline: 071-499 1075.

FRENCH RAILWAYS SNCF

creams/sprays it is a good idea to fit proper insect screens to all caravan windows.

Other than Camping Gaz, the usual LPG cylinders available in the UK cannot be exchanged abroad, so it is advisable to take sufficient gas for the trip. A rule of thumb guide is 1lb a day for normal use. A maximum of three cylinders may be taken on cross Channel ferries so if you are planning a long trip then a combination of your usual gas and camping gaz would be the solution. Remember to have the appropriate regulator as they are not interchangeable.

Mains electricity is provided on Continental sites, although the standards may vary from those in the UK. As this is a potentially lethal facility you should seek professional advice as to the necessary requirements to be followed for safe use. The Information Department of the Caravan Club can advise you.

A foreign touring holiday should be fun and by following the above advice, you will have taken the first steps in preparing for your trip. To get the most out of any holiday, total peace of mind is essential and for that it is advisable to seek the help of the experts, not just for recommended camp sites, but for ferry bookings, breakdowns, and full insurance cover from motoring to medical. The Travel Service of The Caravan Club will provide all these facilities plus the latest Continental Sites Guide and handbooks published this year in two volumes covering not only France and the Med., but also Morocco, Andorra, Eastern Europe, Scandinavia and Cyprus. The world really is your oyster with a caravan.

LET THE TRAIN TAKE THE STRAIN

Covering considerable distances across Europe with your car does not necessarily involve the traveller in mile after mile of driving. There are easier ways of reaching your destination refreshed, relaxed and still have the car to enjoy for the rest of the holiday.

There are numerous motorail services leaving the Channel ports which can take you to the South

French Motorail

of France or the Swiss and German frontiers. It is even possible to book through to Munich from Paris (920 km) or to Madrid from Paris (1458 km).

Many people dismiss the idea of motorail simply because they don't understand the system or because they believe it is far too expensive. However, if you weigh up the cost of motorail against motorway tolls, petrol bills, hotels, restaurants, wear and tear on the car (plus jams, restless children and rows with the wife because she gave you the wrong directions 20 km back)— then motorail wins hands down.

Motorail is simple. Having got your booking, you arrive at the terminal at say Calais or Boulogne, check-in the vehicle and leave SNCF staff to do the rest. You and your family are directed to the passenger train and your couchette or sleeper and you prepare yourself for an enjoyable train experience and a good night's sleep.

While the train eats the miles quietly and effortlessly through the night (and French trains are fast and quiet) you sleep soundly. You awake refreshed the next morning approaching your destination. While your car is being unloaded you find a pleasant Continental style breakfast is awaiting you at a nearby restaurant. The choice is coffee, hot chocolate (or even tea!) Croissants, French bread, butter and jam.

More than 300,000 families take motorail annually, and once bitten families return year after year. Services to Avignon, Biarritz, Brive, Bordeaux and Bologna, Lisbon, Madrid, Milan and Munich are the lure with the reward at the end that having driven from your motorail destination station, you are relaxed and refreshed to continue the journey to wherever. There is an additional service to Rome for 1991.

French Motorail

Sleeping accommodation varies depending on the size of the family — or group — and your budget. There are single 1st class sleeping compartments to six berth couchettes in 2nd class. Sleeper compartments are more like a good hotel room with comfortable beds, washing facilities in the cabin with sheets, a blanket and pillow. The sleeping car attendant will serve drinks on request.

While breakfast is served free of charge courtesy of French Railways, for the onwards travellers packed meals can be purchased at the Motorail terminal or even to be eaten onboard if you purchase at the start of your train journey.

It is easy to book Motorail. You can book through French Railways, 179 Piccadilly, London, W1V 0BA (Tel: 071-409 3518 for information only), your motoring organisations and most travel agents.

Your Motorail booking will also include the Channel crossing if you wish and you benefit from special low rates as a Motorail passenger. Early bookings are advised to ensure space is available at the time you intend taking your trip.

Finally, have you thought about taking the TGV, Europe's fastest train? You can send your car by Motorail while you and your family enjoy the luxury, speed and excitement of this impressive 186 mph (TGV-Atlantique) train. French railways can give you the details, but it is an opportunity well worth considering.

OFF THE BEATEN TRACK

One of the delights of motoring abroad is getting away from the rush of a busy main road and finding a quiet village or restaurant where there are not many people.

It matters little whether you are just motoring around northern France for a weekend, taking a touring holiday through a number of European countries, or indeed heading for the South of France, Spain or Italy. Getting off the Beaten Track adds to the delight of the trip.

There are many unexplored villages to be found within a short distance of "A Class" or motorway systems. Yet year after year thousands of "Brits" drive right past. Some of the best food in France can be found at an Auberge, in Germany at a Gasthof or in Switzerland in a small village restaurant. Not only is the food good, wholesome and usually prepared by a family, but it can be excellent value for money.

Starting in northern France, there is a restaurant "Gare" at the village of Les Attaques. Inexpensive and good food. Just off the same Calais-Saint Omer N.43 road is the village of Ardres and the Hotel Relais offers a very good kitchen. In the other direction in the Vallée de la Course, there are a number of first rate Auberge restaurants offering locally caught trout, excellent steaks and home made pâté. If you like seafood then a visit to the town of Etaples en route to Le Touquet D940 is a must. There is a new quayside restaurant with seafood sold on the ground floor and an excellent restaurant on the first floor.

Just outside Boulogne on the Paris Road N1 at St. Léonard is the Auberge, Le Petit Caporal, which is an excellent family run restaurant offering good low cost meals. There is now a separate hotel opposite offering immaculately clean rooms at 200F for a double. Tel: 01033 2180 3555.

Staying in Belgium but heading towards Luxembourg, it is a "must" to wander through the Ardennes.

An Auberge can often be found in a delightful setting such as this at Lumbres, the Moulin de Mombreux

This picturesque hilly region with quiet villages, small streams and attractive villages offers a wealth of pleasure to those getting away from the main road. There are many restaurants, too numerous to mention, but the choice of food ranges from wild boar to trout, smoked ham and pâté like you are unlikely to taste anywhere else.

Luxembourg is a small country, and I suppose most tourists head for Luxembourg City. Why? — when the best areas are either north east of the city or on the border with Germany. The town of Remish to the south with the River Moselle forming the border is a picturesque small town. Petrol, wines and spirits and many other goods are very cheap here. There are a number of waterfront restaurants offering good food and don't be too deceived by those which look a "tourist trap". They have a lot of people visiting them because they ARE good.

Having crossed the bridge which spans the Moselle River and entered Germany, it would take a book in itself to identify the many villages and restaurants to be tried and enjoyed. However, the famous wine region around Bad Durkheim and Neustadt is an excellent area for small guest houses and restaurants. The lovely village of Saint Martin near Annweiler (famous for the Castle where Richard the Lionhart was held prisoner) offers wine tastings, good quality wine at a "give-away" price and scenery of hills, forests, streams and traditional German architecture.

Move a little further on to the Black Forest region. Near the famous town of Baden-Baden and just to the east of the town of Gernsbach with its river teeming with trout, it's 12th century bridge into the old town, street cafes, restaurants with excellent food and an ideal base from which to

Not an oil painting but the mural on the exterior of a brewery in Bavaria

spend many delightful days touring the "Schwarzwald" region. The Hotel/Restaurant Sonnenhof provides quiet accommodation from it's hillside view of the river and valley and it's restaurant offers good food in tasteful surroundings.

The Bavarian region of Germany is famous and well explored by tourists. Even so there are many small roads leading to pleasing villages which are well of the beaten track. Kotzting, just 12km from the Czechoslovakian border, is hardly known to the Brits and leads to the picturesque towns of Viechtach and Eisenstein. This is the region famous for leaded and cut glass. Restaurant specialities are largely meat based and veal is inexpensive.

South of Munich is the area of Bavaria which is best known. The castle at Neuschwanstein and the town of Garmisch-Partenkirchen with it's many painted houses are well worth visiting, but again outside the main centres there are many village restaurants where prices are more than reasonable.

Switzerland is a country best known for it's mountains and lakes, cows and chocolates. It has a reputation for being expensive. But this probably only applies to the main centres. Wander up some small valley or mountain road, stop at a village restaurant and you will be pleasantly surprised at the quality of food at very reasonable prices. The little town of Zweisimmen in the White Highland region, is one such place. The Hotel Bergmann is an excellent family-run hotel with a good restaurant. On the road from Bern towards Interlaken, turn off right and within 35 miles you arrive. This road then leads to Gstaad,

SINCE 1985, ALL VAUXHALLS HAVE BEEN GREEN

All new Vauxhalls can run on unleaded as well as ordinary petrol or any mixture of the two (except those fitted with 3-way catalytic converters which run on unleaded only). It's no wonder that Vauxhall's pioneering won the first-ever "What Car?" Clean Air Award.

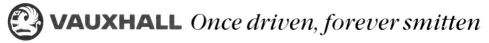

VAUXHALL *Once driven, forever smitten*

GM VAUXHALL IS BACKED BY THE WORLDWIDE RESOURCES OF GENERAL MOTORS. CAR SHOWN CARLTON CDX.

Spend a night in a French Chateau and enjoy an excellent meal in idyllic surroundings. The Chateau du Cocove is just off the N43 Calais/St Omer road

Chateau d'Oex and Bulle. It is a delightful drive through one of the most picturesque regions of Switzerland offering good hospitality, food, cow bells, wood carvings and the chance to buy some famous Swiss cheeses. A cheese fondue is a speciality well worth savouring.

For those heading towards the South of France and missing the delights of Germany and Switzerland, there are still many interesting villages within easy striking distance of the autoroute Sud which are well worth a detour.

For example the **Hotel due Roy — Aisey sur Seine,** route N71 between Chatillon sur Seine and Dijon. Tel: 01033 8093 2165. This small sleepy village in the heart of Bourgogne contains a fine hotel in the beautiful setting of a quiet wooded valley. Although only having ten rooms all are of good quality, comfortable and well furnished. The dining room offers superb meals and the cuisine and service are under the direct supervision of the proprietors Monsieur and Madame Damon; Monsieur Damond is a highly skilled chef.

Although this hotel is ideal for overnight stops, those people "in the know" stay here for two or three days at a time to let the magic of the hotel and it's surroundings enfold them.

Booking well ahead for rooms is absolutely essential. Rooms up to 250FF, meals up to 150FF and a la carte.

Le Cheval Blanc - Sept-Saulx near Reims. Between Reims and Chalons sur Marne on the N44 lies a turning to Sept-Saulx, a small village which contains this fine example of a champagne country hotel. Excellent rooms are complemented by a dining room offering first class cuisine.

The hotel has fine gardens and tennis courts are available. Rooms about 300FF, meals up to 350FF.

The Tonic Hotel du Golf - Cognac. Tel: 01033 4535 4200. As a complete contrast to the other hotels, The Tonic is an ultra modern hotel situated at the Carrefour de la Trache, Chateaubernard at Cognac. However, unlike many of the others, it combines a peaceful and tranquil interior of wood panelling and thickly carpeted corridors with huge bedrooms each containing two double beds and all the latest television services from satellite. Each bathroom is fully equipped with a jacquzzi bath which is ideal at the end of a long day's drive.

The dining room offers good service and sensibly priced meals. This is an ideal hotel for a family to use. Rooms at 290FF, meals to 150FF.

This is just a taste of the countless delights to be found when driving the highways and byeways of Europe. But if you follow the rule that restaurants well patronised by the "locals" are usually good, you will not go far wrong.

AVAILABILITY OF UNLEADED PETROL IN EUROPE

COUNTRY	AVAILABILITY	NOTES
AUSTRIA	Widespread	Regular unleaded (91 octane) available from approximately 1,550 stations.
BELGIUM	Widespread	Premium unleaded (95 octane) available at all petrol stations.
BULGARIA	Limited	Approximately 15 locations
CZECHOSLOVAKIA	Limited	Approximately 15 locations
DENMARK	Widespread	-
EIRE	Widespread	Leaflet available from Touring Information, RAC Croydon.
FINLAND	Widespread	Numerous locations in Southern Finland.
FRANCE UNLEADED: (SANS PLOMB) PETROL: ESSENCE	Widespread	Currently available from almost 1,000 stations. Autoroutes, popular tourist areas. By early July expected to be available from 4,000 locations.
WEST GERMANY	Widespread	-
EAST GERMANY	Limited	Mainly motorways
GREECE	Limited	-
ITALY	Widespread	Available from approximately 5,000 stations at present. Motorways, normal roads and cities.
LUXEMBOURG	Widespread	-
NETHERLANDS	Widespread	-
NORWAY	Widespread	-
POLAND	Limited	Approximately 25 sites.
PORTUGAL	Widespread	Approximately 36 sites, 7 locations on the Algarve.
RUMANIA	Limited	Approximately 10 sites (Petrol coupons not valid for unleaded petrol)
SPAIN	Limited	Available on Motorways in NE Spain. Costa Brava, Costa Blanca, Costa del Sol, Madrid area.
SWEDEN	Widespread	-
SWITZERLAND	Widespread	-
TURKEY	Limited	Available at 34 sites Istanbul, popular tourist areas in S.W. Turkey (e.g. Bodrum, Kusadasi, Izmir)
YUGOSLAVIA	Widespread	Motorways, and especially in Northern Yugoslavia

YOUR GUIDE TO UNLEADED

Unleaded fuel is freely available throughout Europe. However, some countries are more to the fore in this respect than in others, but all garages indicate the availability of unleaded petrol by name.

For example your motoring dictionary should include:

FRANCE: essence sans plomb

GERMANY: bleifrei

HOLLAND: loodvrije

SWEDEN: blyfri

In Yugoslavia the pumps are marked "BMB 95" and in Spain where only one per cent of fuel is unleaded you will find it difficult to spot any difference at all.

Rumania, Bulgaria and Greece are other countries where unleaded is almost non-existent.

If you are heading to Scandinavia, unleaded is certainly freely available in the south.

In Italy unleaded "Super Senza" Pb95, No-AM, Bleifrei" is usually only available on the Autostrade. However, in Switzerland where 50 per cent of all fuel is unleaded the pumps are marked with a green hose and virtually all garages sell unleaded.

Unleaded petrol is on sale in every European country, however, availability does vary from country to country. Availability is continuing to improve in some countries and this information should be used as a guide only.

HOW TO COMPARE PRICES IN LITRES AND GALLONS

APPROXIMATE PRICES		APPROXIMATE VOLUME	
LITRE	GALLON	LITRE	GALLON
33p	150p	0	0
34p	155p	5	1
35p	160p	9	2
36p	165p	14	3
37.5p	170p	18	4
38.5p	175p	22.5	5
39.5p	180p	27.5	6
41p	185p	32	7
42p	190p	36.5	8
43p	195p	41	9
44p	200p	45	10

TOLL ROADS

Motorists can expect to pay in certain European countries for the privilege of driving on motorways and for using alpine road tunnels.

France charges for the use of most motorways, Italy makes a charge and the Swiss make a "once and for all" payment of 30frs for the use of all motorways during a year.

Alpine road tunnels from France to Italy will incur a charge, as indeed will certain Austrian alpine roads and tunnels.

Free motoring can be enjoyed on motorways in Belgium, Holland, Germany, Luxembourg and Scandinavian countries.

WINTER DRIVING

Motoring trips abroad are no longer simply to be taken in the summer months. An increasing number of people now take their car with them on winter holidays, Some to Alpine ski resorts, others in search of the warmer climates offered by France, Spain and Portugal.

Whatever your reason for going abroad with the car from the beginning of December through to April, this section offers you advice and hints based on more than 25 years of winter driving experience.

The first important consideration is whether your car is up to the particular journey you are intending.

Taking the car by Motorail in winter

TOLL ROADS IN AUSTRIA

(All prices in Schillings). Multiple journey cards allow an appreciable reduction in the price charged for a single journey. 20-point cards for category A vehicles cost 800 Sch.
Multiple journey cards can be used on several toll roads and tunnels, as indicated below.

ALBERG TUNNEL (between the Tyrol and Vorarlberg, from St. Anton to Langen)

A1 motorcycle	100
A2 Private car, station wagon, motor caravan, minibus with up to 9 seats, van not exceeding 1.30m. high at the front axle	150
with 20-point card	2 points
A3 A2 vehicle towing a caravan or trailer	210

Card for category A vehicles are valid for one year from their date of issue. Cards for category A vehicles are valid only if the numbered stub or counterfoil is shown when the ticket for a single journey is presented. In other words, tickets may not be detached from the block and transferred to other vehicles.

Cards for category A vehicles are recognised for the Brenner motorway, the Felbertauern road, the Gerlos road, the Grossglockner High Alpine Road, the Pyhrn motorway (Gleinalm and Bosruck tunnels) and the Tauern motorway.

BRENNER MOTORWAY (between the Tyrol and Italy)

	distance covered*	
	whole road	partial section
A1motorcyle	100	40
A2 private car, station wagon, minibus with up to 9 seats, van not exceeding 1.30m high at the front axle, motor caravan	130	50
with 20 point card	2 points	1

***distance covered:** whole road: Innsbrook (East or West) -

Italian frontier; Schoenberg - Matrei, also for short sections.

Cards for category A vehicles are valid for one year from their date of issue.

Multiple journey cards for category A vehicles are recognised for the Alberg road tunnel, the Felbertauern road, the Gerlos road, the Grossglockner High Alpine Road, the Pyhrn motorway, and the Tauern motorway.

FELBERTAUERN ROAD (Salzburg and the East Tyrol)

The Felbertauern tunnel is open throughout the year. It links the Kitzbuhel area with the East Tyrol, thus providing a rapid north-south route through Austria from Munich to Italy and Yugoslavia.

A motorcycle	100
A private car and station wagon	180*
with 20-point card	2 points
caravan or trailer	40

Cards for categories A and E are recognised for the Arlberg tunnel, the Brenner motorway, the Gerlos Road, the Grossglockner and Timmelsjoch High Alpine Roads, and the Pyhrn and Tauern motorways.
**the winter tariff (applicable from 1st Nov to 30th Apr in the following year) for a single journey is 110 S.*

GERLOS ROAD (between Salzburg and the Tyrol)

A motorcycle	50
A private car and station wagon with or without trailer	80
with 20-point card	2 points

Cards for category A vehicles are also recognised for the Arlberg tunnel, the Brenner motorway, the Felbertauern road, the Grosglockner and Timmelsjoch High Alpine Roads, and the Pyhrn and Tauern motorways. Season tickets for the upper section of the Gerlos road are available for motorcycles, private cars and station wagons (not used for the commercial transport of persons) carrying a maximum of 8 persons, as follows:

— for 7 days including the date of issue	240
— for 15 days including the date of issue	320
— for one year (until 31st December of year of issue)	900

GROSSGLOCKNER HIGH ALPINE ROAD

A motorcycle	200
A private car and station wagon with or without trailer, empty coach	250
with 20-point card	5 points

Cards for category A vehicles and cards for coaches are valid for the Arlberg tunnel, the Brenner motorway, the Felbertauern road, the Gerlos Road, the Pyhrn motorway (Category A only), the Tauern motorway and the Timmelsjoch High Alpine Road (Category A only).

PYHRN MOTORWAY (Styria) — (Gleinalm and Bosruck tunnels)

	Gleinalm	Bosruck
A1 motorcycle	100	60
A2 private car, station wagon, minibus with up to 9 seats	130	70
with 20 point card	2 points	1 point or
	2 points for both	
A3 caravan or trailer	40 points	20

Cards for category A vehicles are valid for one year. Multiple journey cards for category A vehicles are valid only if the numbered stub or counterfoil is shown. All cars are recognised for the Brenner and the Tauern motorways. Cards for category A vehicles can also be used for the Arlberg Road tunnel, the Gerlos road the Grossglockner and Timmelsjoch High Alpine Roads.

SILVRETTA HIGH ALPINE ROAD (private cars with caravan trailers prohibited)

per person	30 single	10 same
	day return	
per child 6 to 16 years	10	
child under 6 years	free	

TAURERN MOTORWAY (Salzburg and Carinthia) (upper section)

	distance covered*	
	whole road	partial section
A1 motorcyle	100	50
A2 private care, station wagon, minibus with up to 9 seats		
May to October	190	95
November to April	120	60
with up to 20-point card	2 points	1 point
A3 caravan or trailer	40	20

*distance covered. Whole road: Flachau - Rennweg.
Partial section: Flachau - Zederhaus, Flachau - St. Michael, St. Michael - Rennweg

Cards for category A vehicles are valid for one year from their date of issue. Cards for category A vehicles are valid only if the number stub or counterfoil is shown. Cards for category A vehicles are recognised for the Brenner motorway, the Gerlos road, the Grossglockner and Timmelsjoch High Alpine Roads, and the Pyhrn motorway.

TIMMELSJOCH HIGH ALPINE ROAD (Passo del Rambo)

	single*	return
moped, motorcycle	40	50
private car, with up to 6 seats	80	120
minibus, per person	10	
(but minimum fee per vehicle)	80	

* or tolls to the Timmelsjoch only, when the road is closed - generally from October to May.

Only motorcycles, private cars without trailers and minibuses are admitted on the Italian part of the road. All private cars with luggage or caravan trailers, larger coaches and all types of lorries are prohibited.

Details of tolls applicable for coaches and lorries on major Austrian toll roads and also information on the lesser known toll roads can be obtained from RAC Touring Services Information, Croydon.

If you are going to a ski resort, are the tyres adequate? Have you organised snow chains, because on many roads in the French, Swiss, Austrian and German Alps, snow chains must be carried in the boot, even if they are not required on the wheels!

Has the car been to the garage for a service? Did you tell them the car would be out in temperatures of perhaps -20 C or even lower? Have you had an oil change suitable for winter driving? Is the mixture in the windscreen water bottle of sufficient strength to remain is useful liquid form despite freezing temperatures?

It is estimated that as many as 100,000 British motorists now cross the Channel each winter for skiing holidays. The number is increasing each year as more and more of them discover that it really isn't difficult. Some have been overland before — by coach on a package ski trip — and seen that it really is not difficult to negotiate most European roads in winter.

The benefits are enormous. Put the skis on a lockable roof-rack, pack all the ski boots and extra winter clothing in the boot all from the ease and comfort of your own driveway — and then unpack it when you arrive at your alpine resort hotel. Compare this to those who choose to fly. Limited baggage, some flights not accepting skis, airport delays, even flight diversions and then transfer from the airport half as long as the car journey from say Calais to the nearest alpine ski resort in France!

There are some fairly obvious rules — and some that are not so obvious — about winter motoring. Firstly, drive within your own limitations and those of the car. Drive according to local conditions. If a motorway is free of snow, it might not necessarily be completely free of ice. And if you are driving too fast and have to break quickly, you might find yourself and the car entering the Cresta Run before you have even reached Italy!

If you are on a snow covered surface, then providing you don't attempt to drive too fast and have adequate tyres, then it should not prove too difficult. If the snow has become frozen and rutted, then extreme care is required, and it is useful to fit chains for extra grip.

If you are on a slope covered either by ice or snow, do not try and pull away in first gear or spin the wheels. A slow, very gentle acceleration using 2nd or even 3rd gear will get you moving. Once the car has gained momentum, then you can begin to pull away.

If your purse permits, then invest in two — or even four — winter tyres. They can always be put to good use back home. A very suitable tyre is manufactured in Europe by VERDSTEIN and available through leading tyre garages in England. It has a proven track record in Austria,

Switzerland and Germany and — built more sturdily than a town or country tyre — it can also be studded if required.

Nothing could be simpler. Cross the Channel on a Friday afternoon sailing from Dover by either P&O Ferries, Sealink or Hoverspeed, check-in at the Calais Motorail terminal (located near to the ferry terminal at the Gare Maritime). Your car will be carefully loaded onto a double-deck rail wagon by experienced staff, and you can move to the station restaurant to enjoy a meal before the train departs.

This winter's timetable is as follows:

21.15	Calais Maritime	07.09
09.06	Moutiers	20.00

On arrival at Moutiers station, you leave the train and while your car is being off-loaded, you move to a nearby restaurant where hot coffee or chocolate, hot croissants, French bread, butter and jam is waiting. When you return to the Motorail terminal, your car is waiting — and sometimes even the windscreen has been cleaned by thoughtful French railway staff.

Although this service goes to the heart of the French Alps, it also offers just a short drive into nearby Switzerland without the need for a long car journey all the way from the Channel coast.

Whichever area of the Alps you are intending to visit, go armed for the worst possible conditions. There is an old saying that it is better to be safe than sorry. Alpine roads tend to be narrow and usually with quite a few bends. Don't be lulled into thinking you can imitate the locals. They probably do a mountain climb weekly, if not daily, and they know the road, the next bend and what their driving skill is capable of achieving. Sometimes you can drive up to a resort without any problems. The night before you are due to leave, it can snow "cats and dogs" — well anyway mountains of snow — and even after the snow ploughs have cleared most of it away, you might be crawling down towards the valley in 2nd gear. Having chains on the wheels will give you added confidence and composure, and if it takes ten minutes to take the chains off when you get down the valley, well it's better than hours digging yourself out of a snow drift which you might have skidded into.

A small shovel, a bit of matting are other items worth putting in the boot. An extra bottle of windscreen cleaner that can be used neat if the temperature really falls. A bottle of ice remover is another essential, and if the car door lock freezes, then WD40 or slightly heating the car key and working it in and out of the lock should free it.

Never leave your car parked in freezing conditions with the handbrake on. Always leave it in gear. Leave the car parked — if possible — on a hill facing down just

KILOMETRES INTO MILES

KMS	MILES	KMS	MILES
1	0.62	31	19.26
2	1.24	32	19.88
3	1.86	33	20.50
4	2.48	34	21.12
5	3.10	35	21.74
6	3.72	36	22.37
7	4.34	37	22.99
8	4.97	38	23.61
9	5.59	39	24.23
10	6.21	40	24.85
11	6.83	41	25.47
12	7.45	42	26.09
13	8.07	43	26.72
14	8.69	44	27.34
15	9.32	45	27.96
16	9.94	46	28.58
17	10.56	47	29.20
18	11.18	48	29.82
19	11.80	49	30.44
20	12.42	50	31.07
21	13.04	100	62.14
22	13.67	200	124.28
23	14.29	300	186.42
24	14.91	400	248.56
25	15.53	500	310.70
26	16.15	600	372.84
27	16.77	700	434.98
28	17.39	800	497.12
29	18.02	900	559.26
30	18.64	1000	621.40

THE TIME IT WILL TAKE

It is generally possible to maintain high average speeds on Continental motorways. With this table you can easily check on the average speed, expressed in miles per hour, you need to maintain in order to cover a given distance, expressed in kilometres, in a given time

AVERAGE SPEED

Distance in kilometres	30mph hrs	30mph mins	40mph hrs	40mph mins	50mph hrs	50mph mins	60mph hrs	60mph mins	70mph hrs	70mph mins
20		25		19		15		12		11
30		37		28		22		19		16
40		50		37		30		25		21
50	1	2		47		37		31		27
60	1	15		56		45		37		32
70	1	27	1	5		52		44		37
80	1	39	1	15	1	0		50		43
90	1	52	1	24	1	7		56		48
100	2	4	1	33	1	15	1	2		53
200	4	9	3	6	2	29	2	4	1	47
300	6	13	4	40	3	44	2	6	2	40
400	8	17	6	13	4	58	3	9	3	33
500	10	21	7	46	6	13	5	11	4	26

in case your battery goes flat and you need a "jump start". Doing this forwards is a lot easier than trying to push the car uphill — until you can find a turning circle!

Lockable ski racks are now a legal requirement in some countries. If you are going to invest in a ski rack, then make sure it is lockable. Some journeys require an overnight stop and if the skis are locked on the roof, nobody is going to take them — unless they take the car as well.

A new product on the market is a box which offers complete protection for skis, ski sticks and other skiing equipment. There is only one problem. If you travel Motorail, these boxes are too high to be negotiated with the car onto the rail wagon, and you will be asked to remove the box and put it in the car!

SPIKED AND STUDDED TYRES AND SNOW CHAINS

AUSTRIA — Permitted November 15th to 22nd April only, although special regulations may extend this period and prohibit their use on certain roads. Vehicles up to 3,500 kg. and up to 1,800 kg. axle weight. Speed limit 80 kmh on normal roads, 100 kmh on motorways. All wheels or on 2 wheels if snow chains fitted on drive wheels. Trailer tyres must be studded if towing vehicle has studs. May be used on approved steel radial tyres only. Snow chains can be hired from the Austrian Motoring Club (OAMTC0).

BELGIUM — Permitted November 1st to March 31st. Vehicles up to 3,500 kg. and trailer attached. All wheels except in case of certain slow moving vehicles and trailers of less than 500 kg. Speed 60 kmh on normal roads, 90 kmh on motorways and dual carriageways with at least 2 lanes in each direction. Vehicles with spiked tyres must display a white disc with a red reflectorised border at the rear showing figure "60". Disc should be removed when normal tyres are fitted. Chains may only be used in case of snow or ice.

BULGARIA — Spiked tyres are forbidden. Winter chains and tyres are compulsory where indicated, depending on the amount of snow.

CZECHOSLOVAKIA — The use of spiked tyres is prohibited. Snow chains may only be used when there is enough snow to protect the road surface.

DENMARK — Spiked tyres may be used from 1st October to 30th April. All wheels. NO special speed limits. Chains may be used where necessary, but there is seldom enough snow to warrant their use.

FINLAND — Spiked tyres allowed from 1st October to 30th April. All wheels. Snow chains may be used when conditions make this necessary.

FRANCE — Permitted November 15th to March 15th. Vehicles up to 3,500 kg. Speed limit 90 kmh. May be fitted to RADIAL tyres only. Extensions if weather bad. Chains recommended. In snowy or icy conditions, these must be used where indicated.

EAST GERMANY — Banned on all vehicles whether registered in East Germany or abroad.

WEST GERMANY — Use of spiked tyres not authorised on vehicles registered in West Germany or abroad. However, they may be used by Austrian and foreign drivers in a 15 km wide zone near the German/Austrian border, but they are not allowed on motorways. Chains allowed and for vehicles fitted with these, there is a maximum speed limit of 50 kmh. Snow chains can be hired from the West German Motoring Club (ADAC).

GREECE — No regulations.

HUNGARY — Spiked tyres may be used on snow covered roads. Winter tyres may be used during the year. Snow chains not allowed on private vehicles.

ITALY — In area of Val'd'Aosta, it is compulsory to carry snow chains in vehicles throughout winter until 30th April. Either snow tyres or chains may be used on roads where chains are compulsory. Spiked tyres permitted on vehicles not exceeding 3.5 tonnes from 15th November to 15th March. Mud flaps are compulsory. If spiked tyres fitted, then all wheels including trailers must be equipped. Speed limits: 90 kmh on normal roads and 110 kmh on motorways.

LUXEMBOURG — Spiked tyres allowed from 1st December to 31st March. Special speed limits: 60 kmh in normal roads and 90 kmh on motorways. Snow chains — no regulations.

NETHERLANDS — Spiked tyres not permitted, visitors may use winter tyres or chains. Speed limits must not exceed 80 kmh.

NORWAY — Spiked tyres may be used on vehicles not exceeding 3.5 tonnes from 15th October to 30th April. Special exceptions in the North (Nordland, Troms, Finmark). All wheels, no special speed limits. Snow chains may also be used.

POLAND — Use of spiked tyres ~~are~~ is prohibited; snow chains may only be used on roads covered with snow.

PORTUGAL — Use of spiked tyres is prohibited, but snow chains may be used when necessary.

SPAIN — Only regulations are concerning spiked tyres ~~is~~ that the spikes are at least 10 mm in diameter and the maximum length of spikes is ~~are~~ 2 mm. No regulations in connection with winter tyres and snow chains.

SWEDEN — Spiked tyres permitted 1st October to 30th April. All wheels and those of trailers if used. Radial or winter tyres with extra deep tread advised. Can be used rest of year if conditions require it or if announced by authorities. Snow chains not allowed on main roads.

SWITZERLAND — Permitted November 1st to March 31st or longer if authorised by the Canton. Vehicles up to 3,500kg. and trailers attached. Speed limit 80kmh. Not permitted on autoroutes and semiautoroutes except N13 between Thusis and Mesocco (San Bernardino Tunnel). In areas where chains are prescribed, they must be fitted on at least 2 drive wheels.

USSR — Spiked tyres and snow chains prohibited in USSR.

?? YUGOSLAVIA — Use of spiked tyres prohibited for all vehicles. Driving wheels must be fitted with snow tyres, otherwise all 4 wheels must be fitted with radial tyres. Snow tyres must have grooves with a depth of at least 44mm. If the 4 tyres are summer tyres, chains must be fitted to the driving wheels. Winter equipment is compulsory in Bosnia and Herzegovina between 15th November and 15th March. Elsewhere it depends on roads and weather conditions.

UNITED KINGDOM — No regulations.

Although many countries do not show a maximum speed limit for vehicles with studded tyres, motorists must at all times abide by the laid down speed limits. In certain Alpine countries, chains must be used where indicated.

SNOW CHAINS HIRE OR PURCHASE UNITED KINGDOM

Snow chains can be hired or purchased in the United Kingdom from:-

Selectacar (Touring) Ltd.
10 Plaistow Lane, Sundridge Park, Bromley, Kent, BR1 3PA.
Tel: 081-460 8972/3.

Rud Chains Ltd. 1/3 Belmont Road, Whitstable, Kent, CT5 1QJ.
Tel: (0227) 276611

Snowchains, Bourne Industrial Estate, (also roof boxes and roof racks) Borough Green, Kent, TN15 8DG. Tel: (0732) 884408

Snow chains for purchase only in the United Kingdom from:-
Griff Chains, Quarry Road, Dudley Wood, Dudley, West Midlands.
Tel: (0384) 69415.

DUTY FREE

There are a number of misconceptions regarding the expression "duty free". These days if you acquire an item onboard a cross Channel ferry, it is more likely to be at "shipboard prices" but is probably still cheaper than you would pay in your local high street shop or supermarket.

This certainly applies to spirits such as whisky and gin, it also applies to liqueurs such as Cointreau.

But in other respects it can sometimes be an advantage to shop ashore in countries such as France,

Germany or Luxembourg. Wine is certainly a good buy "ashore" and if you visit a vineyard or a small village in the heart of the winegrowing region of a country, you can buy quality wine at very low prices in comparison to what your local off licence would charge for the same wine — always supposing that you could buy that particular wine back home! Beer is cheap to buy in France and Belgium. You have only to look at how loaded down day trippers are these days with their permitted 8 x 24 bottle cases of beer to realise what a good bargain this is.

Cheese is another good buy. Each European country has its own particular brand — some you may enjoy, others not quite so much. In Holland there is Edam or Gouda, in France Camembert whilst countries such as Germany and Switzerland have a number of varieties depending on what region of the country you are in.

Coffee is another commodity usually a lot cheaper in mainland Europe than in Britain. Why this should be has never been successfully explained but it offers a considerable saving.

Mustard is much sought after and especially the variety of Dijon. Then there are the tinned specialities such as pâté de fois gras (goose or duck

CONTINENTAL AND BRITISH CLOTHING SIZES

CHILDREN'S SHOES

UK	1	2	3	4	5	6	7	8	9	10	11	12	13
CONTINENTAL	17	18	19	20	22	23	24	25	27	28	29	30	31

WOMEN'S SHOES

UK	1	2	3	4	5	6	7	8
CONTINETAL	33	34	35	36	37	38	39	40

MEN'S SHOES

UK	1	2	3	4	5	6	7	8	9	10	11	12	13
CONTINETAL	35	36	37	38	39	40	41	42	43	44	45	46	47

SHIRTS AND COLLARS

UK	14	$14^1/_2$	15	$15^1/_2$	16	$16^1/_2$	17
CONTINETAL	36	37	38	39	41	42	43

MEN'S SUITS AND OVERCOATS

UK	36	38	40	42	44	46
CONTINENTAL	46	48	50	52	54	56

WOMEN'S DRESSES AND SUITS

UK	8	10	12	14	16	18
CONTINENTAL	34	36	38	40	42	44

MEN'S HATS

UK	$6^1/_2$	$6^3/_8$	$6^3/_4$	$6^7/_8$	7	$7^1/_8$	$7^1/_4$	$7^3/_8$	$7^1/_2$
CONTINENTAL	53	54	55	56	57	58	59	60	61

Gloves sizes are usually the same as in the UK. Socks, stockings, etc. where different are measured in cms. not ins.

liver pâté); cassoulet (a stew of bean, pork, sausage and garlic) and confit d'oie (preserved goose). Finally, escargot (snails).

Champagne is certainly a good buy and a visit to the region famous for this will present opportunities not only for making a good purchase but probably a visit to the caves for a tasting. The house of Champagne Pannier at Château Thierry provides tours, tastings and an excellent range of champagne.

One of the least thought of "meccas" for inexpensive purchases is the small country of Luxembourg. Not only is petrol considerably cheaper than elsewhere in Europe but wines, spirits, chocolates, coffee and other items can lead to significant savings. The town of Remisch on the border with Germany is worth at least half and probably a whole day's stop-over in your journey. Useful purchases can be made, fill the tank with petrol and enjoy the many shops and pleasing scenery.

The following table sets out HM Customs Allowances applicable at the end of 1990. No significant changes are expected during 1991 but if in doubt, it is always worth asking on your way through customs. If you do bring back more than your allowance, make sure you travel through the Red Lane "GOODS TO DECLARE". Often it can be as quick and you will find that honesty always pays off.

THE CUSTOMS ALLOWANCES

For goods in each band, you may bring in either the Duty Free or the Duty Paid allowances shown	**DUTY FREE** Goods obtained anywhere outside the EEC or duty and tax free within the EEC eg. from a duty free shop		**DUTY PAID** Goods obtained duty and tax paid in the EEC
Spirits, strong liqueurs over 22% volume Fortified or sparkling wines, some liqueurs	1 litre or 2 litres	**OR**	$1\frac{1}{2}$ litres or 3 litres
Still table wine	2 litres	**OR**	5 litres
Perfume	60cc/ml	**OR**	90cc/ml
Toilet water	250cc/ml	**OR**	375cc/ml
Gifts, souvenirs, other goods	£32 worth but not more than 50 litres of beer 25 mechanical lighters	**OR**	£265 worth but not more than 50 litres of beer 25 mechanical lighters
Cigarettes Cigarillos Cigars Tobacco	200 or 100 or 50 or 250 grammes	**OR**	300 or 150 or 75 or 400 grammes

No-one under 17 is entitled to tobacco or drinks allowances

Countries of Europe A - Z

AUSTRIA

Population: 7.5 million
Climate: moderate climate with temperatures varying depending on location and altitude. Summers can be hot and the evenings cool.

Austria might be a small country but you will need a whole holiday to discover and enjoy the scenic beauty of the country which ranges from lakes to mountains, from the architectural heritage of castles and monastries to the richness of Austria's cultural life.

For the holidaymaker, Austria is a country you can return to time and time again without being bored. Whilst lovers can retrace the lives of Austria's famous composers, others can follow a special route.. "from castle to castle, from palace to palace" which are but two available from the Austrian National Tourist Office in London.

The country is one for the outdoor life. Recreational and

sporting facilities are considerable and if you are wondering how to keep the children occupied, then again the tourist has the answer. A route entitled.. "Also for the Children" which includes attractions which will appeal to the whole family.

AUSTRIA

DRIVING LICENCE — Min. age for UK licence holder to drive temporarily imported car: 18; motorcycle less than 50cc: 16; motorcycle over 50cc: 18. International driving permit recommended.

FINES — On-the-spot.

INSURANCE — Third party compulsory. Trailers must be covered separately. Green Card recommended.

DRINK/DRIVE — 0.08percent limit, but lower levels too if deemed unfit by police surgeon.

LIGHTS — Dipped in poor daylight. Parking lights only in well lit streets at night.

PASSENGERS — No children in front seats less than 12 years without special seat or safety belts. Seat belts compulsory for driver and all passengers if fitted.

SPEED LIMITS — 31mph built-up areas, 62 mph elsewhere. 81mph on motorways.

MOTORCYCLES — Dipped headlights during the daylight and crash helmets compulsory.

SPECIAL FEATURES — Warning triangle and first aid kit compulsory. Special regulations for spiked tyres. Recognised credit cards accepted at many petrol stations.

The Vorarlberg is the province at the western end of Austria bordering Switzerland. Its capital is the lakeside resort of Bregenz with a population of 26,000. There is swimming, fishing and yachting, a cable car to Pfander (1064 m high) and a deer park.

There are also boat excursions on Lake Constance.

Salzburg is a city with a fortress. It's population of 137,830 live in a delightful area of the country and are most welcoming to visitors of many nationalities who flock to the city each year. There are summer festivals in the Hofstallgasse Hall, a toy museum and an old area of the city well worth a visit. Nearby is the Durrenberg salt mine and at Kamprun a power station with nearby water falls and the Kitzloch gorge.

Linz is the capital of Upper Austria and has a most imposing city main square. A visit to the nearby St. Florian Abbey is recommended and there is a funicular to Postlingberg (537m).

At the lower end of Austria is St. Polten with it's Romanesque-Gothic cathedral and a trip along the Wachau Valley by the Danube and the Alpine foothills is a must.

Vienna, the capital of Austria and a population of 1.5m, has to be seen. St. Stephen's cathedral is a delight and a visit to the Schonbrunn Palace is a must whilst in the evening what better way to finish the day than a few hours in the Heurigen (wine tavern). There is so much to see and do in and around Vienna that it is impossible to mention, but a taste of it's delights here. Three days is needed to see everything.

Graz is an old city with a clock tower on the hill and has fortifications, an opera house and Eggenburg Palace. An excursion to

The Cloth Hall at the historic Belgian town of Ypres.
Completely re-built after the devastation of the First World War

the Piber (stud farm of the Spanish Riding School) must not be missed. There are also stalactite caves at Peggau.

Perhaps not too many Brits get to Carinthia and it's Provincial capital of Klagenfurt, but there is plenty to see including a planetarium, zoological gardens and motor boat excursions.

Austria is a beautiful country, full of surprises. Full of mountains and valley scenery, quaint old buildings full of character and extremely friendly people. Food and drink specialities abound. More information of a general or specific nature can be obtained from:

AUSTRIAN NATIONAL TOURIST OFFICE, 30 St. George Street, London, W1R 0AL.
Tel: 071 629 0461

BELGIUM

Population: 10 million (approx)
Climate: 17-23C in summer

For the European motorists who does not want to venture too far then Belgium has richness and diversity to make up any good holiday. From the sandy beaches of the north stretching from the French to the Dutch border, to the forest and rivers of the Ardennes or to the historic cities of Brussels, Antwerp and Liege.

Belgium celebrates many folklore

If you finish up in a town such as Ypres (Belgium) on market day, you could be hard pressed to find your way out! Here a sign indicates "All Other Routes" but there is no other way through

festivals throughout the year. Pageants and events which are steeped in the traditions, legends and history of the country. The dignity of the very moving Procession of the Holy Blood in Bruges should not be missed, like also the famous Gilles of Binche with their baskets of oranges and plumed headdresses. The giants of Belgium are a special feature of the country's folklore and appear in different towns in several places.

The famous Menin Gate at the Belgium town of Ypres. More than 40,000 soldiers with "no known resting place" have their names recorded in stone on the walls

The annual music festivals of Flanders and Wallonia cover all aspects of music with many orchestras and companies taking part. Brussels is the home of the famous 20th century Ballet of Maurice Bejart.

Belgian cuisine is amongst the best in the world. Restaurants abound and you will find a meal to suit your taste. From Seafood to "Carbonnades Flamandes", "Waterzooi" and "Jambomn d'Ardennes" are a few recommendations to try. The beer in Belgium has to be tried. There are over 300 varieties, but beware — Belgium beer can be strong and is not for the driver!

Wallonia is the French-speaking part of Belgium. The Province of Hainaut abounds with old castles and a wide variety of folklore. It's old city of Mons has many fine treasures. Waterloo, south of Brussels, once the scene of a famous fierce battle, now lies peacefully overlooked by the magnificent Lion Mont.

BELGIUM

DRIVING LICENCE — Min. age for UK licence holder to drive temporarily imported car/motorcycle: 18.

FINES — On-the-Spot. Official receipt must be issued.

INSURANCE — Third party compulsory. Green Card recommended.

DRINK/DRIVE — 0.08 per cent limit. Driving licence may have to be surrendered.

LIGHTS — Dipped in poor daylight. Sidelights for parking in poor visibility.

PASSENGERS — No children under 12 in front seats. Seat belts in front compulsory.

SPEED LIMITS — 35mph in built-up areas. 56mph elsewhere. 74mph on motorways.

MOTORCYCLES — Dipped headlights during daylight compulsory. Visitors recommended to wear crash helmets.

SPECIAL FEATURES — Warning triangle compulsory. Special regulations for spiked tyres. Diners Club International and Visa at some petrol stations.

The Ardennes comprise dense forests, winding rivers and picturesque castles with footpaths meandering over the hills and through the river valleys. On the banks of the Meuse are the towns of Namur and Dinant and make good centres from where you can explore the famous grottoes of Han and Rochefort.

The German-speaking section of Belgium is centred around Eupen. In the south, Bouillon with it's celebrated castle perched high above the town, huddles around the banks of Semois.

Belgium may be a small country (30,500 square kilometres), but it has a fine network of motorways (toll-free) and you can move from one area to another quickly. For example, you can leave the coast near Ostend and be on the border of Luxembourg in less than three hours!

Despite being caught up in the conflict of two world wars, Belgium people are friendly and welcome visitors. For real atmosphere of the past and Belgium's troubles, visit Ypres and see the battlefields of the First World War, the preserved trenches and how the buildings and famous Cloth Hall in the centre of the town have been re-built in traditional style.

So despite it's size, Belgium has much to offer and many secrets to reveal. For further information, write to the:

BELGIUM NATIONAL TOURIST OFFICE, 38 Dover Street, London, W1X 3RB. Tel: 071 499 5379

CZECHOSLOVAKIA

Population: 15.5 million
Climate: Prague (winter -4 - +1C) (summer +14 - +25C)

Since October 1st last year British visitors no longer require a visa for entry, opening up the delights of this central European country. With a road network stretching 74,000 km (46,250 miles) motorists can discover the eventful past and interesting present in this country.

Scenery ranges from mountains to valleys and forests and to lakeside resorts. Most people visiting Czechoslovakia for the first time will want to see the capital, Prague. The centre of cultural events, castles, history and gastronomic delights rolled into one.

For the traveller touring throughout this land there are good accommodation and catering facilities. This ranges from luxury hotels included in international hotel chains to motels, chalet camps and auto-camps. There are agencies where accommodation can be booked in advance or at any of the Czechoslovak travel offices.

There is a network of 1060 petrol filling stations and of those, 915 are open on Saturdays and 635 on Sundays. Unleaded 91 octane petrol is available.

Traffic regulations and road signs are the same in principal as those in most other European states. Motorists are not permitted to park on main roads or on forest roads. Drinking and driving is forbidden and children under the age of 12 cannot travel in the front seat.

There is little doubt that with the opening up of Czechoslovakia more British will be heading "east". The easiest access by car will be through Germany crossing at Rozvadov, Folmava, Zelezna Rude, or Strazny. It is then about 150 km (93 miles) to the Czech capital.

Further information can be obtained from:

CZECHOSLOVAK TRAVEL BUREAU - CEDOK (LONDON) LTD. 17-19 Old Bond Street, London, W1X 3DA. Tel: 071 629 6058

DENMARK

Population: 5.1 million
Climate: Average in Copenhagen -3.2C in February: 14-22C in July.

Denmark is the Southern most of the Scandinavian countries covering an area of 16,600 square miles which includes the Jutland peninsula and more than 400 islands (100 of which are inhabited).

There are good beaches to be found almost anywhere and the coastline is 2,800 miles in length. There are no mountains or rivers, but scenery is forever changing with hills, forests and lakes.

Motoring in Denmark is a pleasure and even the smallest of secondary roads are ranked amongst the best in the world. Signposting is really good and you can venture off main roads without fear of getting lost. Motorways are free and speed limits should be strictly observed. Even with minor motoring offences, drivers can face a heavy on-the-spot fine. Failure to pay can mean your car is impounded.

Getting around Denmark will usually mean at some stage you need to take a ferry, certainly to get to the main island and Copenhagen you will have arrived by ship. But ferries are comparatively inexpensive and services are frequent. Indeed they run like local bus services and there is no booking requirement. You just arrive and take the next available service.

Denmark is a country rich in sightseeing for tourists. Perhaps the

DENMARK

DRIVING LICENCE — Min.age for UK licence holder to drive temporarily imported car/motorcycle: 17.

FINES — On-the-Spot.

INSURANCE — Third party compulsory. Green Card recommended.

DRINK/DRIVE — 0.08 per cent limit.

LIGHTS — Dipped headlights recommended in poor daylight visibility.

PASSENGERS — Recommended that children do not travel in front seats. Seat belts compulsory in front seats.

SPEED LIMITS — 31mph built-up areas. 49mph elsewhere. 62mph on motorways.

MOTORCYCLES — Dipped headlights compulsory in daylight. Crash helmets with straps compulsory.

SPECIAL FEATURES — Warning triangle strongly advised. Special regulations for spiked tyres. Give way to traffic approaching from the right. Some recognised credit cards accepted at petrol stations.

most famous these days and important for family holidays, is a visit to Legoland located at Billund on the Jutland peninsula. It is an adventure park with models of space stations, airports, castles and palaces. For the children there are rides on trains, roller-coasters, monorail, boating or simply drive your own Legoland car.

These are scenes of magnificant buildings throughout France worth visiting

For adults, Jutland provides many castles, windmills and museums. Augustenborg Castle was built for a Duke in the 1770s and is now a hospital. Grasten Castle is the summer palace of the Danish royal family, and the changing of the guard can be watched daily at 11.00 hours.

The town of Esberg in West Jutland is a major fishing and commercial port and has a fisheries and maritime museum. Varde is worth a visit to see the well preserved houses and the old port of the town produced in miniature.

West and central Sealand is a region of manor houses, interesting

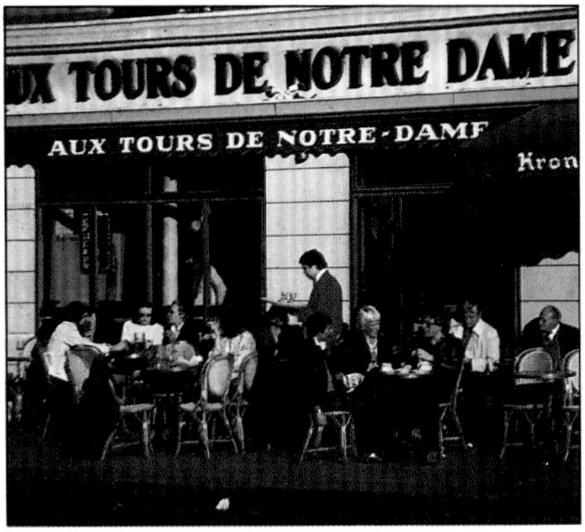

Pavement cafes are a familiar scene throughout Paris

churches and rolling countryside. The Merlose Church is one of the oldest and most interesting in Denmark. It was built around the year 1100 AD and at Farevejle Church, the Earl of Bothwell, who was husband to Mary Queen of Scots, is buried.

Odense is the birthplace of Hans Christian Anderson , and a visit to the museum to see the living rooms and personal effects of this famous fairytale writer are worthwhile.

In Copenhagen itself, the famous Tivoli Gardens are a must and a visit to the Harbour to include a boat trip to get a better view of the Little Mermaid, the fishing harbour and the picturesque old buildings of Christianshaven.

Holidays in Denmark are not cheap, but good value for money can be obtained by staying at Danish inns. It is an association of 66 of the best ins all over Denmark. Details of this and other tourist opportunities can be obtained from:

THE DANISH TOURIST BOARD, 169/173 Regent Street, London, W1R 8PY. Tel: 071 734 2637

FRANCE

Population: 55.8 million (approx)
Climate: Summer (south) 28C
Summer (north) 21-22C

France is a country for lovers! So say the French, but you don't have to be on your honeymoon or celebrating an anniversary to enjoy

Parc Asterix just north of Paris is a family paradise offering a full days' enjoyment at a reasonable price

all that this country has to offer.

It offers an unlimited choice of gastronomy, night life, sports and art. All wrapped up in it's capital — Paris. But elsewhere in France, there is a richness of everything which makes for a successful holiday. The Loire Valley and it's castles, the Alpine region with skiing, fishing and magnificent views, the south with superb beaches and warm sunshine or the great lakes of the Champagne-Ardenne region.

These are scenes of magnificant buildings throughout France worth visiting

To British people, the Champagne region means only one thing — Champagne to drink! But south of Reims and en route to Troyes, you discover first the Der-Chantecoq Lake, covering an area of 4,800 hectares (48 km2) and 10 km at it's widest. The lake is the biggest artificial lake in Europe and the largest stretch of water in France.

To the east lies the Orient Forest Lake covering an area of 2,300 hectares, and is soon to be complimented by the new lakes of Auzon and Amance. It is a favourite spot for lovers of peace and quiet and water sports. Sailing, windsurfing, water-skiing, canoeing and fishing.

Near the great lakes you can discover another side of the region. The Champagne route takes the traveller past vines, through numerous towns and villages indicated by the name plates "commune appellation champenoise" (towns within the official Champagne wine growing area).

A trip through this region is worthwhile not only for it's charm, but also for it's variety. You can dream, relax and — for the non-driver — taste some wine!

The town of Troyes is the historic capital of Champagne and throughout the changing fortunes of history has managed to maintain an artistic and historic heritage of outstanding richness. The cathedral's stained glass windows, the House of Tools, the Marinot glassworks and the Museum of Modern Art.

If you are a sun seeker, then the South of France with it's famous resorts of St. Tropex, Nice, Cannes, etc., will tempt you. France has 2000 miles of coast not all of it so well known. South of Brittany near Bordeaux stretches along a beach of 125 miles lined with sand dunes.

A French seaside resort offers tables on the pavement, cool beer, seafood and sunshine. All for a perfect holiday

CALAIS - traditional landfall for generations of British travellers bound for the Continent and far and away the best route today. Modern jumbo car ferries plus giant hovercraft provide a choice of over 100 crossings daily during the summer and never less than 50 off peak. Take the shortest crossing between Dover and Calais. From 75 minutes by car ferry and from 30 minutes by hovercraft.
DOVER
Calais
- the shortest route to France

From 75 minutes by car ferry and from 30 minutes by hovercraft

The most pleasant part of this coast extends from the charming small village of Hossegor all the way to the Spanish border. The Atlantic Ocean breakers provide excellent sport for surfers and stimulating dips for bathers.

The town of Villejuif depicting the straight line of the RN7

The area also provides golf courses, horse riding, forests and a climate which is gentle in winter and temperate in summer.

People associate mountains with snow. Snow with skiing and therefore mention the French Alps, and you immediately think of the perfect winter, providing the best skiing resorts in Europe. Perhaps not always the most attractive — but at least with the best runs and facilities. But spring, summer and autumn can also be the right time for a holiday in the mountains. There is golf, fishing, swimming, flights around the Alps and yes — even summer ski resorts. Take your camera and your binoculars for a visit to the Parc de la Vanoise des Ecrins or du Vercors for the flora and fauna, see if you can spot the chamois and if you find edelweiss, do not pick it, but savour it's fine perfume.

For a real treat visit a local restaurant and taste local specialities such as cheese fondue, air-dried beef, country ham or delicious blueberry tart.

There is so much to France that we can only wet your appetite for more. So why not write to the

FRENCH NATIONAL TOURIST OFFICE,
178 Piccadilly, London, W1V 0AL.

FRANCE

DRIVING LICENCE — Min.age for UK licence holder to drive temporarily imported car/motorcycle: 18; motorcycle less than 80cc: 16; more than 80cc. 18.

FINES — Severe on-the-spot fines. Official receipt must be issued.

INSURANCE — Third party compulsory. Green Card recommended.

DRINK/DRIVE — 0.08 per cent limit.

LIGHTS — Dipped in poor daylight.

PASSENGERS — No children under 10 in front seats. Seat belts in front compulsory.

SPEED LIMITS — 37mph built-up. 56mph elsewhere. 68mph on dual carriageways with central reservation. 81mph on motorways. In wet weather limits outside built up areas down to 49, 62 and 68mph. Drivers with less than a year's experience 56mph limit.

MOTORCYCLES — Dipped headlights in daylight compulsory for bikes over 125cc. Crash helmets compulsory.

SPECIAL FEATURES — Warning triangle or hazard warning lights compulsory. Set of spare bulbs advised. Special regulations for spiked tyres. Traffic entering roundabouts has priority unless indicated otherwise.

Boulogne, France: Picturesque Harbour Scene

GERMANY

Population: 80 million (approx.)
Climate: 21C (North) 25C (South) average in summer, winter -5C (East)

Unification of the "two" Germanys last October means this is now the largest country within Europe. The immediate effect of the reunification is the opening up of the eastern half of this country adding an additional 108,333 sq. km. of territory and the opportunity to freely visit Berlin, Leipzig and Dresden.

Germany boasts one of the finest motorway systems in Europe extending over 9,000 kms. The country is about 500 miles from north to south and now stretches from the French/Belgian frontier to the west and to Poland in the east. For the motorists it offers something for every mood.

Vineyards, woods, lakes, rivers and mountains, castle, beaches and lots of sunshine.

For those who like activity holidays, there is swimming in both

(Left) The impressive spire of Köln Cathedral. Whilst much of this German city was destroyed in the Second World War, the Cathedral escape the worst damage and much of the brickwork is currently being restored. (Below) Ornate ironwork signs often hang outside butchers, restaurants, dairies and fish shops. Although these can be found throughout Germany, they are most popular in Bavaria.

indoor and outdoor pools, fishing, boating, yachting, climbing, tennis, horse riding, skiing and excellent walking tours through forests and valleys.

A horse drawn carriage provides a relaxing way of sightseeing at Garmisch-Partenkirchen

Finding a starting point, or even somewhere as a base is difficult, because the visitor is spoiled for choice. Many British people head for Bavaria and some opt for the region south of Munich, and towards the

Bavarian towns and villages are famous for the murals on buildings

rivers and mountains. But eastern Bayern in the Bayerischer Wald is an area yet to be discovered by the British. A growing number of Dutch people, the comparative cheapness of accommodation and restaurants and the delightful villages with their painted exteriors, cleanliness and quietness.

Travellers to Germany can find excellent guest house accommodation in villages "off the beaten track"

The Bayerischerwald is east of a line from Nurnberg and Munich and extends to the border with Czechoslovakia. In winter, the area has a very good snow record with a number of ski resorts located on mountains of about 1,000m. high. In the summer rivers abound with trout, and there are lakes also offering good trout fishing. Licences average 10/12 DM a day (£3/£4) and the sport is excellent. You are usually allowed four fish and those you catch above this number you pay by the kilo.

Regensburg is about 50 miles

north of Munich and traces it's roots back to the first century AD. The city has a fine cathedral, a 12th century stone bridge and a palace of the princes of Thurn. Shopping is also good. Nurnberg (Nuremberg) is a mainly modern city which has retained it's medieval centre. It has an imperial castle, a city wall over 3 miles long and a museum of toys.

Between these two cities are many attractive villages worth visiting, including Lam, Kotzting and — if you are interested in glass — then a visit to Bodenmais and Arnbruck is a must. Not only do they make fine lead crystal glass on the premises, but they have shops which sell glassware at ridiculously low prices. A decanter and six glasses could cost you as little as £40!

Many restaurants in small German villages offer excellent value for money. They can be picturesque on the outside, clean and friendly inside

The main street in the old part of Garmisch-Partenkirchen in Bavaria

Many people think the north of Germany is industrialised. So it is in parts, but the real north around Hamburg is really attractive. Schleswig-Holstein is Germany's "little Switzerland" and the dukedom of Lauenburg. The undiscovered towns of Ratzeburg and Molln are

Summers spent on the continent mean coffee on the patio or in the courtyard of a country restaurant

worth a visit or to the beach at Travemunde. North Germany also has a number of small islands which are summer resorts and, given to good weather, are superb.

Touring Germany should include the Rhein and the vineyards of the Rheinland Pflaz. First visit the riverside city of Koblenz and either follow the Mosel river or the Rhein. Small villages on the Deutsche Weinstrasse such as Saint Martin or Gonnheim have numerous small vineyards where they sell by the litre quality wine at between £1.10 and £2.00 a bottle!

A visit to the enlarged Germany could not be complete without such places as Berlin, Potsdam or Dresden. In the "Nicholas Quarter" of Berlin the street organ players or

Street organs can still be found in many German towns. This young lady is trying to raise funds for less privalged children

to Dresden to see the famous Semper Opera House. The countryside is spectacular, and the Wernigerode Castle in the Harz Mountains is special. Winter sports here are good as indeed they are in

The "Disney like" Castle of Neuschwanstein in Bavaria

The architecture in some German towns, especially in the Black Forest area, is quite outstanding ánd well worth venturing "off the beaten track" to see

the Ore Mountains. At Potsdam the unique Sans Souci Palace still has it's original Rococo interior and, of course, this is the city nominated as the royal residence in the late 17th century.

Finally, the southern area of Germany best known probably by most British people, extends to the Alps through true Bavaria. Garmish Partenkirchen is, of course, famous, as are the numerous castles, including Schloss Neuschwanstein. Lakes such as the Ammersee and Starnberger see both south of Munich are good for swimming, fishing and yachting.

Striking architecture in the old town area of Köln. Some houses in the old town date back to 1235.

GERMANY

DRIVING LICENCE — Min. age for UK licence holder to drive temporarily imported car/motorcycle: 17.

FINES — On-the-spot. They can be levied for bad language, making derogatory signs or running out of petrol on a motorway.

INSURANCE — Third party compulsory. Green Card recommended.

DRINK/DRIVE — 0.08 per cent limit.

LIGHTS — Dipped in poor daylight. Driving on sidelights only prohibited.

PASSENGERS — No children under 12 in front seats. Seat belts compulsory for driver and all pasengers if fitted.

SPEED LIMITS — 31mph built-up areas. 62mph elsewhere. Recommended motorway and dual carriageway max. 81mph.

MOTORCYCLES — Crash helmets compulsory.

SPECIAL FEATURES — Warning triangle compulsory. Use of spiked tyres prohibited. Slow moving vehicles must stop and let others pass. Few petrol stations accept credit cards.

Further general information on the country of specific details of any particular area of Germany can be obtained from the:

GERMAN NATIONAL TOURIST OFFICE 61 Conduit Street, London, W1R 0EN. Tel: 071 734 2600

HOLLAND

Population: 14 million
Climate: 17C Summer 1 to -4C Winter

The Netherlands (often referred to as Holland) has an area of 42,000 square kilometres. It is best known for it's clogs, windmills and flower bulbs. But the motorist can discover the "other Holland" from national costumes and cosy seaside resorts to castles and baroque style churches.

The Netherlands Tourist Office provides an excellent motorist's map, and contained on the reverse in addition to motoring regulations, lists of hotels and roadside restaurants, there is a whole variety of routes that will take the visitor on a journey of exploration through this attractive landscape.

Not all of Holland is flat, although a considerable proportion is. For centuries the Dutch have been

Holland is famous for tulips and windmills

fighting to keep the sea at bay. They have even successfully reclaimed vast areas of land from the sea by the construction of huge dykes, some of which you can drive over with your car. An eerie, but spectacular experience.

There are some of the lesser known regions of Holland, an example being on the Belgium/German border where a small 'splinter' of Holland runs through some fine and varied scenery.

The region of Limburg on the river Maas has a 2,000 year old culture with the oldest city in The Netherlands — Maastricht — and the oldest coal mine in Europe — Kerkrade. It is a province full of natural beauty and interesting sights.

Maastricht is rich in buildings of the Middle Ages. In the St. Petersberg, there is a very old labyrinth of passageways. At Eijzden, there is a picturesque castle and two 17th century watermills. At Vaals where Holland, Germany and Belgium meet, the town is situated on the highest hill in Holland (322m). Valkenburg offers caves, catacombs, model coal mine, cable railway and fairytale wood.

Wherelse but Holland!

Amsterdam, the city of diamonds

Zeeland and the south of Holland islands provide great estuaries, sleepy towns in the world — the Delta project. Middelburg is the capital of the Province of Zeeland and has Gothic town hall and miniature village. Sluis was the former seaport of Brugge on the now silted-up Zwin. It has city walls with three gates and a unique Dutch belfry dominating the town.

No visit to Holland can be complete without sampling the delights on offer from the large cities of Amsterdam, Rotterdam and The Hague. Each has a character of it's own not to be missed.

Rotterdam is the world's largest seaport, which can be visited by river tour. Amsterdam with it's waterway system is a delight whilst The Hague is a charming, friendly town and an ideal seaside resort.

Delft pottery, the tulips and daffodils offered by Frans Roozen at Vogelenzang south of Haarlem or a visit to one of the theme parks for the children such as at Duinrell (Wassenaar) can all be included in the itinerary.

Cheese festival in Holland

Only by visiting Holland can the motorist appreciate the wealth of attraction which is on offer. To get a taste of what is in store, write for further information to:

NETHERLANDS BOARD OF TOURISM, 25-28 Buckingham Gate, London, SW1E 6LD.
Tel: 071 630 0451

HUNGARY

Population: 10.6 million
Climate: Continental with Mediterranean and Atlantic influences Coldest month January -1 to +2C average. Hottest month July +22C average

British visitors to Hungary have not required a visa since October 1 of last year. This now opens up the delights of this small, but attractive country which borders Austria, Yugoslavia and Czechoslovakia. Cultural events include folklore programmes, festive weeks, open air performances and concerts with one of the most important being the Budapest Spring Festival in March.

For the outdoor enthusiast Hungary offers fishing, horse riding, hunting and water sports. And for those looking for spa treatment, then this is a country renowned for being rich in medicinal and thermal waters. The Danubius Hotel and Spa company operates a chain of hotels which provide high quality accommodation and medical care.

For those who enjoy touring, then Hungary's road network provides an excellent link of 30,000 kilometres. The letter "E" denotes you are on a European road network. "M" denotes motorways and highways. In Hungary you can visit the famous Lake Balaton south west of Budapest. This is the largest freshwater lake in Europe of 600 km2. Or some of the many picturesque small villages. There are over 500 museums, but not many towering mountains. The highest peak is Kekes in the Matra mountains at 1,014m. Two thirds of the country consists of plains below 200m. in height.

The capital, Budapest is two cities nestling on either side of the Danube River.

BUDA, the hilly side, offers a wonderful view of the Castle District with it's cobbled streets, Fishermen's Bastion, Matthias Church, Spa and Royal Palace. Take a ride on the chair lift or the Pioneer Railway up the Buda hills.

On the opposite side of the Danube is PREST, the modern metropolis and business centre with it's shops, department stores and vibrant main street complete with trams. Budapest certainly offers something for every taste with a range of good restaurants offering traditional or international cuisine.

A tour of western Hungary can include the ceramic collection of Margit Kovacs museum in Szentendre, the medieval town of Visegrad or the largest cathedral in Hungary located at Esztergom. The

Baroque town of Gyor is also worth visiting. Then there is Count Szechenyi's Castle at Nagycenk or Sopron, one of the oldest cities in Europe.

For those with a special taste the Champagne winery at Boglarlle should not be missed or for those with a romantic sense, how about gypsy music in the Mattias Cellar back in Budapest.

There are many thousands of service stations throughout Hungary which are mostly run by AFIT, but in nearly all main towns you can find Shell.

Motoring regulations in Hungary conform to the Vienna and Geneva Transport Conventions. But remember, NO DRINKING AND DRIVING IS PERMITTED AT ALL. Car horns can only be used if there is danger of an accident. Dipped headlights must be used from dusk to dawn and children under the age of 12 must not travel in the front seats of cars. You must also NOT pass a tram stationary at a stop and there are ON THE SPOT fines for contravening traffic regulations.

Further information from:

HUNGARIAN NATIONAL TOURIST OFFICE, 35 Eaton Place, London, SW1. Tel: 071 235 7191

No visit to Italy is complete without seeing Venice

ITALY

Population: 57.3 million
Climate: Summer (north) 24C
Winter 4 to -11C

Italy stretches from it's northern Alpine region through the Italian Riviera to the southern tip of the country, and the resorts of Cisternino, Acquafredda, Maratea and Alba Adriatica.

Using motorways in Italy can be expensive as they are toll roads. Milan-Naples will cost 15,500 lire for an average family car, whilst Turin-Trieste is priced at 9,500 lire and Florence-Pisa is 6,000 lire (1989 prices). However, the motorist can obtain a petrol concession worth up to 15 per cent on current prices AND a discount of motorway tolls by obtaining vouchers before departure. The Italian Tourist Office offers four schemes, one for northern Italy, one for Central Italy and two for southern Italy. Cost varies from £67.30 (1989 prices) to £189.40, but each is designed to provide adequate petrol and motorway vouchers — and save the tourist a considerable amount of money.

Whilst petrol vouchers are a must, the holiday motorist to Italy does not have to necessarily use the fine motorway system. It depends where

A boat trip to an island can be a journey into the past

The Italian lakes have many villages constructed on the side of surrounding hills

you are travelling and how quickly you want to move from one area to another. However, a package is recommended.

There is an abundance of things to do and places to visit in Italy. Yachting, fishing, horse riding, golf and skiing (even summer skiing!). There are botanical gardens, safari parks, spas, opera, music and drama festivals, museums, art galleries and archaeological sites.

The regions of Italy vary enormously. The Aosta Valley in the north has several high mountains, including Mont Blanc and Monte Rosa with unspoilt scenery of forests and wild flowers. A cheese fondu (Fonduta) is a speciality dish of the region or Vitello Valdostana (veal chops stuffed with soft cheese). Both can be washed down with local wines which include Pinot gris, Donnas and Enfer D'arnier.

Piedmont (Turin) is a fertile land at the foot of the mountains and is a region rich in lakes. It boasts elegant baroque architecture and excellent cuisine with a strong French influence. Turin is an elegant city with many important museums. Lake Maggiore offers a mild climate and quiet atmosphere. Venice is a "must" on any visit to Italy and is considered by many to be the most beautiful city in the world. Some of the famous

Architectural treasures await the visitor to Italy

Spectacular views of Swiss mountains can be achieved by those fit enough to enjoy the climb to higher pastures

Venetian villas can still be visited. Veneto was the name originally given to this north-eastern part of the Po valley which includes the beautiful range of the Dolomite Mountains.

ITALY

DRIVING LICENCE — Min. age for UK licence holder to drive temporarily imported car: 18. (if top speed less than 112mph) or 21 (where more than 112mph). For motocycles: 17 — less than 125cc., 18 — between 125cc and 250cc., 21 — over 350cc. Italian licence translation required with green UK licence, but not for pink.

FINES — On-the-spot. Heavy for speeding and parking offences. Receipt must be issued.

INSURANCE — Third party compulsory for cars and some boats. Green Card recommended.

DRINK/DRIVE — Strictly forbidden. 0 per cent allowed.

LIGHTS — Use of full headlights in towns prohibited. Dipped lights compulsory in tunnels.

PASSENGERS — Recommended that children do not travel in front seats. Seat belts not compulsory.

SPEED LIMITS — 31mph in built-up areas. Then according to engine size. 49 to 68mph elsewhere and 56 to 86mph on motorways.

MOTORCYCLES — Crash helmets compulsory.

SPECIAL FEATURES — Warning triangle compulsory. Special regulations for spikes and chains. Replacement bulb set recommended. Visa at some petrol stations.

Emilia Romagna lies between Lombardy and Tuscany, and is a rich and fertile land broken by pleasant hills. The Adriatic coast has lively international resorts such as Rimini, Riccione, Cattolica and Cesentatico and all within easy reach of the tiny republic of San Marino on top of the majestic Mount Titano.

Speciality dishes include pasta, tortellini, ravioli, prosciutto (parma ham) and ciliege di vignola (cherries). The best wines are Lambrusco and the strong Sangiovese.

Florence, set on the banks of the Arno, is one of the finest cities in the world and contains many art treasures. Then — like much of Italy — there is much treasure and beauty for the tourist to rediscover.

Whichever region of Italy is your choice, or perhaps a touring holiday to include much of what has been written about, then contact the

ITALIAN STATE
TOURIST OFFICE,
1 Princes Street, London, W1R 8AY.
Tel: 071-408 1254

LUXEMBOURG

Population: 370,000
Climate: Summer average 13 to 23C
Winter1 to -2C

The Grand Duchy of Luxembourg is an independent sovereign state with the present monarch, the Grand Duke Jean succeeding to the throne in 1964. He has a cabinet of 12 members, but the legislative power rests with a Parliament of Deputies.

The population is about 370,000 and the country comprises of about 1,000 square miles. A third of the country is covered by forests and geographically it can be divided into two. The northern uplands of the

The Moselle River which separates Germany and Luxembourg at the border town of Remisch

Ardennes which are hilly and scenically beautiful, whilst the south enjoys rolling farmlands bordered on the east by the grape growing valley of the Moselle.

Luxembourg enjoys many gastronomic specialities from black pudding (treipan) and sausages, smoked pork with broad beans, Ardennes ham which is sliced paper-thin and served raw to calve liver dumplings served with sauerkraut and boiled potatoes. Any of these can be washed down with Luxembourg's own beer or wine from the Moselle region. The country's wine industry can offer a range of white wines to enchant and intrigue the most exacting tastes.

Although it is a comparatively small country it is worth more than a fleeting visit. Many items in Luxembourg are much cheaper than elsewhere in Europe. Petrol and diesel for example, spirits and surprisingly, many restaurants, although you are recommended to "shop around".

For those who enjoy outdoor pursuits, there is horse riding, golf, tennis and there is a considerable network of marked paths for walking tours.

Tourist attractions include a number of museums and castles including the Grand Ducal Palace in Luxembourg which can be visited from mid-July to the beginning of September daily except Wednesdays and Sundays.

Amongst the chief places of interest are Beaufort (409 metres high) situated in Luxembourg's "Switzerland" with it's modern castle and imposing 12th century ruined castle. Berdorf is one of the main tourist centres and is located on a vast tableland overlooking the valleys of the Black Ernz, and Sure and the Aesbach.

Clervaux is situated in a deep and narrow valley beside the River Clerve in the midst of the Ardennes and has a Benedictine Abbey, and interesting parish church in the Rhenish-Romanesque style and 85 km. of well marked walks.

Esch-sur-Sure is a small, typical Ardennes market town and lies in one of the most impressive settings

There are many restaurants at Remisch where you can sit and enjoy a coffee or a beer, have a meal and watch steamers on the Moselle River sail past

in Luxembourg between deep crags and almost completely surrounded by the River Sure. On a high rock was once a mighty castle. The town is reached by passing through a tunnel constructed in 1850.

LUXEMBOURG

DRIVING LICENCE — Min. age for UK licence holder to use temporarily imported car/motorcycle: 17.

FINES — On-the-spot. Unauthorised parking can result in car being impounded.

INSURANCE — Third party compulsory. Green Card recommended.

DRINK/DRIVE — 0.08 per cent limit.

LIGHTS — Sidelights required for parking where no streetlights. Compulsory to flash headlights at night when overtaking outside towns.

PASSENGERS — No children under 10 in front seats. Seat belts compulsory in the front seats.

SPEED LIMITS — 37mph built-up. 56mph elsewhere. 74mph on motorways

MOTORCYCLES — Dipped headlights during daylight and crash helmets compulsory.

SPECIAL FEATURES — Warning triangles compulsory. Special regulations for spiked tyres. Visa accepted at many petrol stations.

Wherever you travel within the Grand Duchy, you will find a welcome and unexpected delights. Do not overlook this small, but picturesque country.

Further information can be obtained from:

LUXEMBOURG NATIONAL TOURIST OFFICE,
36/37 Piccadilly, London, W1V 9PA.
Tel: 071 434 2800

SPAIN

Population: 38.8 million
Climate: (North) Summer 18 to 22C. (South) Summer 26 to 28C.

There is far more to Spain than it's famous seaside resorts, increasingly populated throughout the summer months by the peoples of Europe.

For the motorist taking a holiday in Spain, there is the opportunity with a carefully chosen and well-planned holiday of the opportunity of discovering something quite special. In landscape and climate there is considerable variety to be found. From the mountains of the Pyrennes to the mountains of the Sierra Nevada. From Bilbao in the north to Malaga in the south, there is beauty, rugged landscape, great rivers, vineyards, fruit orchards and pastureland.

Spain has five great rivers, but only one flows into the Mediterranean. The Tajo at 1,000km. is the longest and stretches from the Montes Universales to Lisbon in Portugal. The Ebro (910km.), the Duero (895km.), The Guardiana (778km.) and The Guadalquivir (675km.) vary from fast flowing and — in parts — used as canals to mere trickles of water and at times of the year are completely dry.

Spain provides watersports enthusiasts with placid lakes and rapids on rivers. For the fisherman there are salmon and trout to be found.

SPAIN

DRIVING LICENCE — International Driving Permit (IDP) compulsory for green UK licence holders unless accompanied by Spanish translation. IDP not compulsory for holders of pink licences, but is still recommended. Min. age for UK licence holder to drive temporarily imported car/motorcycle (over 75cc.): 18.

FINES — On-the-spot. Receipt should be issued.

INSURANCE — Third party compulsory. Green Card strongly advised. Bail bond recommended. NB: Bail bond may not be acceptable without Green Card.

DRINK/DRIVE — 0.08 per cent limit.

LIGHTS — Dipped headlights compulsory on motorways and fast dual carriageways. Full headlights in built-up areas prohibited. Use sidelights or dipped.

PASSENGERS — Children not recommended for front seat travel. Front seat belts compulsory outside built-up areas and Madrid ring road (M-30).

SPEED LIMITS — 37mph built-up areas. 56mph outside built-up areas. 62mph on 1st category roads. 74mph on motorways.

MOTORCYCLES — Dipped headlights during daylight compulsory. Crash helmets compulsory.

SPECIAL FEATURES — Set of replacement bulbs compulsory. Warning triangle recommended. Two triangles compulsory for vehicles with more than nine seats. Credit card payment for petrol not available.

Spain's enormously varied climate and extreme geography has allowed a fascinating and diversified plant life to evolve. From the Alpine wild flowers of the high Pyrennees to the tropical date palms of the south, a whole spectrum of trees, flowers, herbs and fruits can be discovered.

A few thousand years ago the whole of Spain was largely covered with forest. By building boats and houses, collecting fuel the population has eaten away at the woodland. There is now an extensive programme to once again introduce large areas of forest.

In the north west of Spain, the pilgrim's cathedral of Santiago de Compostels and it's multi-windowed sister in Leon are well worth a visit. The coastline of Asturias and the deep inlets of Southern Galicia provide fine beaches and spectacular views. Galician cooking is excellent and renowned for it's seafood.

In busy fishing hamlets women make lace by day, men sail their boats out in the evening and in between, the visitor can find green pastures with dairy herds, Austrian apple orchards and chestnut and oak trees.

In the north west of Spain are the sophisticated summer beaches offered by San Sebastian and Santander. Cornis Cantabrica offers small resorts, fishing ports and deserted beaches and at Santillan del Mar a Cantabrian village has been conserved in it's entirety as a national monument. The prehistoric cave paintings at Altamira are only 2km away.

The north east has spa resorts, two national parks and, of course, it's famous ski resorts in the Pyrenees. There is fishing, riding, tennis and golf in this, Spain's second most populated region. Although summers tend to be busy, particularly on the coastal stretches, spring, autumn and

A train journey through Switzerland provides an ideal way of enjoying the scenery of mountains, lakes and forests

Lake steamers provide a "bus" service to allow visitors the chance to enjoy the delights of the scenery and attractive villages

winter tend to be quiet and good times for a visit.

Spain may be a long way for the motorist. But consider going at least one way by French Motorail from the Channel coast. Spain has many fine motorways, also excellent and quiet "A" class roads. You can enjoy the landscape and varied scenery that only a motoring holiday to Spain can bring.

For further information on the country or a particular region of Spain write to:

SPANISH NATIONAL TOURIST OFFICE,
57-58 St. James Street, London, SW1A 1LD. Tel: 071 499 0901

SWITZERLAND

Population: 6.4 million approx
Climate: Summer average 21C
Winter -3 to +2C

Situated in the heart of Europe with it's climate influenced by the ocean from the west and by Continental land masses, Switzerland is a paradise for any holidaymaker.

For the motorist, Switzerland is easy to reach by either the French motorway system from Calais to Strasbourg or by way of the Belgian and German motorways. As a contribution towards their excellent motorway and alpine bridge system, the Swiss levy an annual tax of 30SFs. You can purchase the vignette (windscreen sticker) at either

The only way to the top of Schynige Platte near Interlaken is to walk — or to take the mountain train

the border crossing or preferably from the AA, RAC or Swiss National Tourist Office in London before you set out on your journey.

Two thirds of Switzerland consists of snow-covered mountains, ice, rock, forest and Alpine pasture. Only a quarter of the country is arable, yet it has established a world-wide reputation for it's cheese, chocolate and clocks.

Switzerland has a reputation for other things that are also good. Holidays certainly. People from all parts of Europe head for this tiny country throughout the year and the British rank very high on the annual list of most visitors. There is no lack of interesting things to do. The country has over 600 museums, parks and zoos and there are annual festivals, traditions and games for the visitor to enjoy. Sport abounds from sailing and fishing, canoeing and swimming, even river rafting, gipsy caravan holidays and horse riding.

Probably most British people visit Switzerland to see the lakes, mountains and valley scenery and providing you stay out of the main centres, hotels and restaurants are moderately priced so your holiday need not cost too much.

Lake Thun and the Lake of